Southampton

at War 1939–45

Your Towns and Cities in World War Two

Southampton

at War 1939–45

John J. Eddleston

Pen & Sword
MILITARY

First published in Great Britain in 2017 by
PEN & SWORD MILITARY
An imprint of
Pen & Sword Books Ltd
47 Church Street
Barnsley
South Yorkshire
S70 2AS

ISBN 978-1-47387-054-3

Typeset by Concept, Huddersfield, West Yorkshire HD4 5JL.
Printed and bound in England by CPI Group (UK) Ltd, Croydon CR0 4YY.

Pen & Sword Books Ltd incorporates the imprints of Pen & Sword Archaeology,
Atlas, Aviation, Battleground, Discovery, Family History, History, Maritime,
Military, Naval, Politics, Railways, Select, Social History, Transport, True Crime,
and Claymore Press, Frontline Books, Leo Cooper, Praetorian Press,
Remember When, Seaforth Publishing and Wharncliffe.

For a complete list of Pen & Sword titles please contact
PEN & SWORD BOOKS LIMITED
47 Church Street, Barnsley, South Yorkshire, S70 2AS, England
E-mail: enquiries@pen-and-sword.co.uk
Website: www.pen-and-sword.co.uk

Contents

CHAPTER ONE

1939

By the dawn of 1939 citizens throughout Britain knew that they were living in difficult and threatening times and that the future was most uncertain. Adolf Hitler had come to power in 1936 and it soon became clear that he had expansionist designs outside the German Reich. He consolidated his position over the next few years and in March 1938, the *Anschluss* combined Austria with Germany. This in itself did not satisfy Hitler and it was soon evident that he had ambitions concerning other territories.

On 30 September 1938, the Munich Agreement was signed by Germany, France, the United Kingdom and Italy allowing Hitler to annex the Sudetenland. The end of the year saw the infamous *Kristallnacht pogrom* and the increase in the persecution of the Jews. Many people in Britain knew where all of this would inevitably lead, even though they hoped fervently that war with Germany might be avoided.

In Southampton, 1939 opened with news of a local hero – with four legs! Don, a 5-year-old Dalmatian, lived with his owner, Mrs Wheeler, in Rushington Lane, Totton and on New Year's Day he saved his mistress's home, and his own life.

Mrs Wheeler, a teacher, had gone out leaving Don alone in the house. A nice fire was burning in the grate and, apparently, one of the coals fell out and started a fire on a mat. Don jumped onto a chair, took the catch of a steel-framed window in his teeth, pulled it down, opened the window and jumped out into the street, barking furiously. This attracted the attention of Mr Matthews who lived next door and, going to check what all the fuss was about, saw smoke coming from the house. He then dashed back into his own house, collected a fire extinguisher and brought the blaze under control. The walls and ceiling of the room were blackened and an armchair was destroyed, but there is no doubt that Don's action had saved the day.

Don, the dog who saved his owner's home in January 1939.

Just a few days later, there was news of another local hero and this too was a dog. Rough, an 8-month-old terrier, had barked loudly and raised the alarm when thieves broke into Mr Bradley's tobacconist shop on Commercial Road. The noise frightened the intruders and the potential thieves escaped empty handed. Rough was given a large juicy bone as a reward.

It was also during the first few days of the year that two privates, William Bradley and William Davis, both of the Royal Army Medical Corps (RAMC) and based at the Royal Victoria Hospital in Netley, appeared in court charged with being drunk and disorderly, close to the hospital. The offence had taken place on 30 December 1938 and after being told that they were to be arrested, both of the soldiers assaulted Constable Dolby. For that offence, both men received prison sentences of three months.

It seemed that Southampton docks was not the safest place to be in the first month of 1939. On 11 January, five men were injured in an accident when a motor launch on the boat deck of the Cunard White Star liner *Aquitania*, berthed at the Ocean Dock, fell from its moorings onto the deck striking a number of men working beneath. Michael Costello and Noel Gibson escaped physical injury but suffered the effects of shock. Harry Fluellen sustained head injuries whilst William Ahern suffered a number of fractured ribs. The fifth man, David Kennedy, hurt his left shoulder. Fortunately, all the men eventually made a full recovery.

Later in the same month, the local populace read of a tragic accident at the docks. Arthur Edward Meech of White's Road, Bitterne, was employed as a shunter for the Southern Railway. On 13 January he was riding on one of the buffers of a wagon that was being shunted by an engine named *Honfleur*. The engine was pushing the wagon towards Millbrook when a taxi, driven by William John Oakley of Bryanston Road, also in Bitterne, passed in front of the wagon. The rear end of the cab just caught the wagon where Meech was standing which caused him to lose his balance and fall onto the line. The engine then ran over him, killing him instantly. An inquest, lasting two days and ending on the 21st, returned a verdict of accidental death.

There was further drama at the docks on the 26th when a massive 60-ton crane crashed, trapping the driver, 64-year-old Alfred James John McGregor. Workmates had to tear open the cabin and extricate McGregor before a fire could engulf him. Rushed to hospital, he was found to be suffering from an injury to his right shoulder, a wound on his forehead and burns on his right arm. Fortunately for him, the crane had toppled onto the dock itself. Had it fallen the other way, into the water, McGregor would certainly have drowned.

There had been a great fall of snow in Southampton on Saturday, 28 January and many people were sheltering in doorways, trying to avoid the worst of it. One such person was 54-year-old Alice Lottie Watts of 2 Landsdowne Road, Millbrook. She was in the town centre, in the doorway of the Royal Anchor Hotel in Commercial Road, at around 10.00pm, waiting for her bus to arrive.

Seeing the bus approaching, Alice dashed out into the foul weather but had only gone a few steps when she slipped on some slush and fell face-first onto the pavement, cracking her forehead in the process. Some people had seen the accident and went to Alice's aid. She was

The collapsed crane which buried Alfred McGregor at the end of January 1939.

picked up and taken into the Royal Anchor where she was given first aid but it was clear that she would need specialist treatment so she was taken to the hospital where she lost consciousness so was then admitted. Her husband, an ex-policeman named William, was playing in a police band at the Guildhall where there was a Burn's Night dance taking place. He was summoned to the hospital and was at Alice's bedside when she passed away at 1.00am the following day.

A very sad story was revealed in the police court at the end of the month. Mabel Carvley, aged 40, of New Road, was charged with the attempted murder of her two sons, Richard and Edward. She was also charged with attempting to take her own life.

Edward Carvley, aged 11, told the court that on 18 January he, his brother and his mother had all gone to live in one room at 12 New Road. He slept with his mother whilst his brother slept on a couch. A few days later, on 21 January, he had woken at 6.00am and detected a smell of gas. Thinking nothing of it, Edward went back to sleep and woke up again at 8.00am. The smell of gas was stronger now and he felt sick. By that time his mother was awake and he asked her if the gas was on. She went to the gas tap and said that it was on a little bit. She turned the tap off, opened a window, got dressed and went out. Later that day, the police came to the house.

Richard Carvley, the elder of the two boys at 12 years, said that he too had woken at 8.00am. He could smell gas and noticed that the tap had been turned out by about an eighth of an inch.

Dr Hugh John Trenchard said that he had examined Mabel at the hospital later in the morning of the 21st. He could find no evidence of gas poisoning but she was confused and rather hysterical.

Alice Robinson worked as a cleaner at the Ministry of Health offices in East Park Terrace. She testified that Mrs Carvley had approached her at about 8.40am on the 21st and said that she needed a doctor. She was in a distressed state and close to fainting. The police were called after Mrs Carvley had admitted that she had turned the gas on in the room where she lived.

Constable Burns was the first officer on the scene. He detected a strong smell of gas. The gas tap was now turned off, the window was open about 4in and both the boys seemed to be well. Later, Mrs Carvley made a statement in which she said, 'I tried to gas my youngsters. They woke up and I had to turn the gas off.'

The case was adjourned for a week whilst medical reports and further inquiries were made. When Mrs Carvley made her second appearance, on 6 February, the court ruled that there was no point in continuing with the prosecution as this had all been a temporary aberration. The prisoner was discharged and thanked the court, from the dock.

At the beginning of February, a special police guard had to be set up at Southampton airport. Telephone calls had been received and a voice speaking in broken English had stated that the hangar would be fired. A search of the airport was made but nothing suspicious was discovered. In addition to the police patrol, the nightwatchmen were told to be especially vigilant. Officials believed that the calls were a hoax but no chances could be taken.

At the end of February, a report appeared stating that South-ampton was the premier port in the kingdom when it came to pas-senger numbers. The town dealt with no less than 47 per cent of all passenger traffic and was also placed number four on the list of cargo ports. This implied, of course, that if war with Germany ever did come, Southampton would be a major target for the enemy.

A theft from a motor car took on greater significance at a case heard in the police court on 6 March.

On 25 February, Edward Joseph Doyle had taken a leather case from a car belonging to Alexander Mackay Morrice whilst it was parked in Winn Road. Unfortunately, Alexander Morrice was a medical gentleman and the black leather case contained a hypodermic syringe and some very dangerous drugs including morphine, strych-nine and digitalin.

The loss was reported to the police the same day and such was the concern of the authorities that a radio appeal was broadcast, asking the public for help. This was heard by Walter Stoner, a lodging-house keeper in Portland Terrace. He saw Doyle, one of his lodgers, with a case which had the name 'Morrice' emblazoned on the front. Stoner asked Doyle how he had come by the case and he replied that a friend had given it to him in the street. Nevertheless, Stoner advised Doyle to take the item to the police.

Doyle did take the case to the police and repeated his story of a friend handing it to him. The story was investigated and found to be untrue, leading Doyle to be charged with theft. Once he was in court, however, Doyle not only admitted this theft but asked for two others to be taken into consideration. He was sentenced to three months' hard labour.

Meanwhile, in Europe, Hitler was creating even more problems. On 15 March, Germany occupied the remaining part of Czechoslo-vakia in violation of the Munich Agreement. A few days after this, in Southampton, a curious family case was heard by the magistrates on the 21st.

James Charles Lines, a 58-year-old blacksmith of Marine Parade, was charged with ill-treating his 12-year-old daughter, Edith. He was charged with causing her grievous bodily harm on 12 March. Edith explained to the court that on that date she had gone to her sister's house and had returned home at 5.30pm. Her step-mother asked where she had been and Edith replied, 'For a walk.' Her step-mother then hit her and sent her to bed. Rather than obey, Edith left home again and didn't return until 9.30pm when she was escorted there by two police officers who had found her wandering the streets. When her father came home and heard the story he slapped her across the face and also about the shoulders and head, and then kicked her in the side.

James denied ever kicking his daughter. He explained that he had been married three times and had a total of fifteen children. He admitted that he had lost his temper but swore that he had only hit her with his bare hands.

The court, it seems, was rather on the side of the father, stating that there might be far less juvenile crime if parents administered proper discipline to their children. It was true that the defendant might have gone a little further than he had intended but there was no need to administer any penalty and James was discharged. On the same day that James had appeared in court, Hitler demanded the return of the Free City of Danzig to Germany. War seemed to be moving ever closer and on the last day of the month, the UK and France offered a guarantee of Polish independence. If Poland was invaded by Germany, the UK and France would declare war.

On 1 April, the Spanish Civil War finally ended with victory for General Franco, who appointed himself dictator. The following week, on 7 April, Mussolini invaded Albania. The threat to peace was growing and, perhaps coincidentally, on the same day that Italian troops invaded, it was reported that gold valued at £8 million had left Southampton, on board the American liner *Washington*, bound for New York. Some £6 million, stored in 500 boxes, was loaded at Southampton, the remaining £2 million having already been loaded aboard the ship in Le Havre.

The next day, 8 April, 19-year-old Walter Martin appeared in court at Southampton to answer a charge of persistently importuning for an immoral purpose. The offence had taken place in Kings Terrace, Southsea on 10 March and Martin, of 16 Fling Street, also in Southsea, was bound over for one year and sternly warned as to his future behaviour.

It appeared that those in government were certainly expecting war to come and preparations were being made, not just for military action, but also for support within the UK itself. Thus, on 11 April, the Women's Royal Naval Service, or Wrens, was formed.

In the third week of April, the 20th to be precise, Adolf Hitler celebrated his 50th birthday in Germany. There were widespread demonstrations of affection throughout the Reich and King George sent a telegram of congratulations from Windsor Castle. Five days later, on the 25th, Southampton had a greater reason to celebrate for the Civic Centre was finally completed. The official opening took place the following day, 26 April, when the Duke and Duchess of Gloucester officiated. Two days later, on the 28th, Herr Hitler made a speech in the Reichstag confirming that he did not want war with the UK. Whether that was believed or not, the country still prepared for war. On 27 April the Military Training Act was passed, though it would not actually come into force until early June. This introduced conscription and, to begin with, all men aged 20 and 21 would have to undertake six months of military training.

An 11-week-old mystery was finally solved on the morning of 5 May when a badly decomposed body was recovered from the water off the Royal Pier. The body was identified, by means of its clothing, as that of 37-year-old Francis Stephen Liddell who had vanished from his lodgings at St Michael's House on Saturday, 18 February.

Mr Liddell was reported missing by his sister, Mrs Horne of 17 Bedford Place, on 14 March. She had also informed the police that

The new Civic Centre, opened in April 1939.

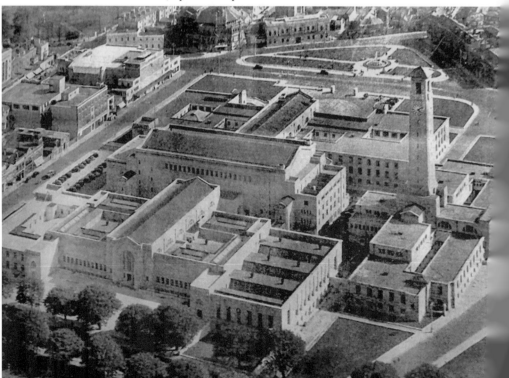

The Duchess of Gloucester at the opening of the Civic Centre.

her brother's 12ft dinghy was absent from its berth at the Royal Pier. That vessel was found a few days later, in the waters off Hythe.

Mrs Horne was also able to tell the police that Francis had been very depressed since his twin brother, Reginald, had recently passed away after a long illness. It had been William Penman who identified the body of Francis, but only because he recognised the suit as one he had passed on to Francis some time before.

It was, of course, for the coroner to rule on whether this was a case of suicide or misadventure. Since no note had been left, an open verdict was finally returned.

There was a curious postscript to this tragedy for on the very next day after Francis had been taken from the water, another badly decomposed body was found in the Ocean Dock off Berth 46. This too was the body of a man and the only description possible was that he had been bald and had been wearing grey tweed trousers, a white shirt, underpants and socks. He had a gold signet ring on one finger which had the initials 'E.G.' engraved upon it. He also wore gold cufflinks. Despite this, the poor man was never identified.

On 13 May, what should have been a straightforward court case turned into something rather different.

Testing barrage balloons in Southampton before war was declared.

Harry James Sirl was a London postman who had been summoned to appear on a charge of non-payment of maintenance to his wife Vera, who lived in Southampton. The warrant was in the sum of £206.6*s*. Payments had been set at 17*s*.6*d*. per week but no payments had been made since August 1935 and it had taken Vera some time to trace her husband so that the summons could be served upon him.

At one stage, Sirl was asked to explain his circumstances so that a new order could be made and to this he calmly replied, 'I have committed bigamy.' Vera Sirl, who was present in court, paled and had to be assisted into a chair. As a result of his statement, Sirl was told that he would be handed over to the Metropolitan Police.

The King and Queen were also in the news in May. On the 17th they arrived in Quebec to make the first ever visit to Canada by a reigning monarch. The trip would also include a visit to New York.

At the end of the month, on 22 May, the Pact of Steel, known formally as the 'Pact of Friendship and Alliance between Germany and Italy', was signed by Fascist Italy and Nazi Germany. The Pact declared that there would be further cooperation between the two powers, but in a secret supplement the Pact is detailed as a military alliance. If war came, Germany and Italy would fight together.

On 1 June, the submarine HMS *Thetis* had been lost whilst on trials in Liverpool Bay. By the 3rd all hope for the ninety-nine men on board had been abandoned and it was on that day that the *Southampton Echo* reported that one of the dead was a local man, Stanley Stevens, who had lived at 22 Weymouth Terrace and was an only son.

Back in Southampton there were reports that the long summer was continuing. It was now twenty-one days since there had been any rain in the town. On the 8th there had been storm clouds over the town and intermittent rumbles of thunder but still the weather hadn't broken. The maximum temperature registered in Southampton was 86 degrees and there had been 11 hours of continuous sunshine. Unfortunately, the newspaper had apparently tempted fate for within a few days the thermometer had dropped, the heavens had opened and the rain had come down in torrents.

On 22 June the royal family returned to Britain after their trip to Canada and the US. They sailed into Southampton on *The Empress of Britain*, escorted by motor torpedo boats and passenger craft. The local populace turned out in great force to greet them and a large 'Welcome Home' banner was hoisted across the junction of the Western Esplanade and Herbert Walker Avenue.

Six days after the royals returned to England, on 28 June, the Women's Auxiliary Air Force was formed and three days later, on 1 July, the Women's Land Army, to work in agriculture, was set up. These were yet more preparations for a war that might come soon.

Another sad case opened before the Southampton Coroner in July. An extract from an army officer's letter to his mother was read at the court on 5 July. It began, 'By the time you get this, I am afraid I will be dead. I cannot go on any longer.'

The letter had been written by Lieutenant Vere Kingsley Butt of the Dorsetshire Regiment who had been found hanging in his cabin on board the troopship *Lancashire*, in Southampton docks. Lieutenant Butt had just been appointed as adjutant for a voyage to India and back.

Evidence was given by the dead man's mother, who lived in Bournemouth. She had last seen him on the day of his death when she said goodbye to him at the railway station where he caught a train

In June 1939, the royal family returned to Britain via Southampton after a trip to Canada.

Crowds lining the streets to mark the return of the royal family.

to Southampton. She reported that her son had been suffering from depression for the past six weeks or so and he had told his sister that he did not feel competent enough to take on his new duties. It appeared that this had preyed on his mind and evidence was given that Lieutenant Butt had gone to his cabin on board the ship, had stood on his trunk, placed a cord around his neck and jumped off. The coroner recorded a verdict that death was due to self-hanging, and that at the time the balance of the young man's mind was disturbed.

It was also in July, on the 10th, that the Prime Minister, Neville Chamberlain, reaffirmed the UK's support for Poland. He made it clear that the UK would intervene on behalf of Poland if hostilities broke out between them and Germany.

At 5.30pm on the evening of Thursday, 27 July, a 63-year-old widow, of Northumberland Road, died in the Royal South Hants and Southampton Hospital from burns she had suffered whilst trying to make herself a cup of tea.

Mrs Lucy Filleul had only been a lodger at Northumberland Road for three weeks and occupied a room on the ground floor. At about 9.30am on that Thursday she had put the kettle onto the gas-ring and hadn't noticed that her pinafore had touched the naked flame and caught fire. She then sat down on her bed, causing that too to catch fire. Soon she was engulfed in flames.

Lucy ran to the door and tried to get out of her room but she had locked the door and, in her distress, was unable to open it. She called out for her landlady, Mrs Amelia Smith, who was in her kitchen downstairs at the time. Amelia asked what the matter was and Lucy replied, 'I am alight.'

Without hesitating Amelia dashed outside, went to Lucy's window and threw it open. Inside she saw the poor woman engulfed in flames and called out for her to get to the window. Lucy managed to do that and Amelia then pulled her out, sustaining extensive burns to her own hands and arms in the process. She then put Lucy down onto some ferns and called out for another lodger, Miss Laura Agnes Davis, to bring some carpets or rugs. Miss Davis did so and then these were used to smother the flames. Mrs Smith then brought some water and, despite being injured, managed to douse the curtains which had caught fire as she pulled Lucy out. Neighbours arrived and helped to put out the fire in the rest of the room.

The inquest on the dead woman took place the following Saturday, 29 July, when the coroner gave praise for Amelia's brave action. All Amelia could say before she burst into tears was, 'I only wish I could have saved her life.' A verdict of accidental death was duly returned.

George William Hollis was a ranger in the New Forest and on Friday, 18 August he was on a routine patrol when he found a saloon car parked in an area known as Braydon Oak Bottom. Even as he approached the vehicle he feared the worst because he could see a rubber tube stretching from the exhaust pipe to the interior of the car. Those fears were realised when he looked inside the car for there was a young couple and both were dead.

They were both sitting in the back of the car and the man had his arm around the girl whose head was resting on his shoulder. The police were called and after examining the scene were able to put names to both. The man was 23-year-old Arthur David Oliver and the woman with him was Peggy Rosina Matthews who was just 21. The pair had both been citizens of Southampton, Arthur residing at 213 Upper Hill Lane and Peggy at 35 Pentire Avenue, Shirley.

The investigation showed that the couple had been sweethearts for about two years and when the families were interviewed it became clear that Peggy had been totally devoted to David but his feelings for her might not have been as strong, though he was still deeply attached to her.

Peggy had worked as a telephonist for Tote Investors Ltd of 20 Portland Street and when her boss, Mr Scholes, was spoken to he confirmed that she had been at work on Tuesday, 15 August, when she had seemed her normal and happy self. Mr Scholes had been away from the office on the Wednesday and when he returned on Thursday the 17th he found that Peggy had not been into work. He had assumed that she must be ill and was surprised she had not contacted the office to confirm that.

David's father, William, had no idea that his son had been any-where near Southampton recently. David had worked for the Survey Department of the Royal Engineers and had been stationed in Kent. He also said that David was the youngest of his four children.

No note had been left by the couple, though the police had found the ashes of a burnt letter next to the car in the forest. It was clear that the couple had taken their own lives but no one had any idea as to why they had done so.

War drew ever closer in August. To the great surprise of the Allies, on 23 August, the Molotov-Ribbentrop Pact was signed between Germany and the Soviet Union. It contained secret provisions for the division of Eastern Europe; the joint occupation of Poland; and Soviet occupation of the Baltic States, Finland and Bessarabia. This pact removed the threat of any Soviet intervention if Germany should decide to invade Poland. Exactly a week later, on the 30th, Germany sent an ultimatum to Poland concerning the Polish Corridor and the Free City of Danzig. War was close and as a result of the German ultimatum, the Royal Navy proceeded to war stations.

On 1 September, without waiting for a response to its ultimatum of the previous day, Germany invaded Poland. On the same day, Estonia, Finland, Latvia, Lithuania, Norway and Switzerland all declared themselves to be neutrals. The UK government declared a general mobilisation of the British armed forces. The same day, Operation Pied Piper began a four-day evacuation of children from London and other towns and cities which were believed to be targets for German bombing. One of those towns was Southampton and many children were sent to the safety of the countryside.

On the same day that all this was happening across Europe, an inquest took place at Southampton, into the death of 76-year-old John Alfred Aitchison of New Road. A number of schoolboys had been playing on Southampton common when they noticed Mr Aitchison sitting on a bench. There was a sudden movement and then the gentleman stood, walked forward and entered a pond. One of the boys ran for help and found Sapper Howard Mumford, a native of Weymouth. Having heard what had happened, Mumford immediately threw off his coat and plunged into the water. He managed to pull Mr Aitchison back to dry land and noticed that there was a deep wound in his throat. Later, a blood-stained razor was found in bushes some 440yds from the pond. Medical evidence was given that the wound in the throat was the cause of death and Mr Aitchison's landlady testified that he had been ill and depressed for some time. A verdict of suicide whilst the balance of his mind was disturbed was returned.

On 2 September, Britain and France issued a joint ultimatum to Germany, demanding that they should immediately evacuate Polish territory. On the same day, the National Service (Armed Forces) Act 1939 was enacted and this enforced full conscription for all males aged between 18 and 41.

COUNTY BOROUGH OF SOUTHAMPTON.

GOVERNMENT EVACUATION SCHEME

EVACUATION

WILL TAKE PLACE ON FRIDAY & SATURDAY, SEPTEMBER 1st and 2nd

THE SCHEME COVERS ONLY—

Schoolchildren (private, elementary and secondary).

Teachers and registered helpers.

Children under 5 if they are accompanied by the mother, or some other adult in place of the mother.

Expectant mothers.

Blind persons and cripples (not chair cases).

All those who are in these classes and wish to be evacuated, whether they have given their names in or not, MUST report at one of the assembly points given below, at the time and on the day stated.

Note: 1.—In the case of a family which has schoolchildren the assembly point should, if possible, be one of the schools at which the children attend, otherwise it should be the nearest school.

2.—A schoolchild who comes to school on the day of evacuation for that school will be evacuated. If you do not want the child to go, keep him or her away from school.

3.—Be in time.

4.—Bring gas-mask, food for the journey and a change of clothes. One bag only for clothes.

1st day.	Friday, Sept. 1st, 1939	2nd day.	Saturday, Sept. 2nd, 1939
Bitterne Park Boys	Not Later Than 6.0 a.m.	Highfield C.E. Swaythling Senior Girls	Not Later Than 6.0 a.m.
Bitterne Park Infants Freemantle Boys, Girls and Infants Ludlow Road Boys, Girls and Infants Mount Pleasant Girls and Infants Northam Infants St. John's St. Anne's Secondary School	Not Later Than 6.30 a.m.	Bassett Green Infants Bassett Green Junior Boys Foundry Lane Girls and Infants Springhill R.C. Boys, Girls and Inf. Swaythling Infants Western District Boys and Girls Atherley School for Girls Grammar School for Girls King Edward VI School Taunton's School	Not Later Than 6.30 a.m.
Ascupart Girls and Infants Bevois Town Boys, Girls and Infants Bitterne Park Girls Bitterne C.E. Infants Bitterne Manor Deanery Boys and Girls Eastern District Boys and Infants Merry Oak Pear Tree Green Sholing Girls Woolston Boys, Girls and Infants Woolston R.C. Itchen Secondary School	Not Later Than 9.0 a.m.	Aldermoor Junior Mixed Central District Boys Chestnut Road Boys Coxford Girls Foundry Lane Boys Laundry Road Infants Portswood Girls and Infants Regent's Park Boys and Infants St. Denys Boys, Girls and Infants St. Jude's C.E. St. Mark's C.E. Swaythling Senior Boys	Not Later Than 9.0 a.m.
Bitterne C.E. Boys and Girls Mount Pleasant Boys Northam Boys and Girls St. Joseph's R.C. St. Mary's C.E. Sholing Boys and Infants Station Road	Not Later Than 12 noon	Aldermoor Infants Central District Girls and Infants Portswood Boys Regent's Park Girls Shirley Infants, Junior Boys and Girls Shirley Warren Senior Boys and Girls Western District Infants	Not Later Than 12 noon

IF YOU ARE NOT BEING EVACUATED, WILL YOU PLEASE KEEP WELL OUT OF THE WAY AT THE ASSEMBLY POINTS AND THE RAILWAY STATIONS.

ASSEMBLY POINT FOR BLIND PERSONS AND GUIDES — 43, THE AVENUE On FRIDAY, SEPTEMBER 1st, at 9 a.m., Ready for Immediate Evacuation.

War had yet to be declared but notices were posted detailing the early evacuation of children.

The fateful day was 3 September. The Germans had not replied to, or complied with, the joint British and French ultimatum. As a result of this, at 11.15am Neville Chamberlain made his famous speech on the radio stating that the deadline for the withdrawal of German troops from Poland had expired at 11.00am and that 'consequently

Southampton children practising their gas-mask drills.

this nation is at war with Germany'. Within hours of the broadcast, Australia, India and New Zealand also declared war on Germany. This was followed, on 6 September, by South Africa joining the Allies in declaring war.

Things were moving very rapidly now. On 7 September, the National Registration Act introduced identity cards and allowed the government to control labour. Two days after this, on the 9th, the British Expeditionary Force crossed to France. The next day, Canada also declared war on Germany. One week later, on the 17th, the Soviet Union invaded Poland and on the same day the aircraft carrier HMS *Courageous* was torpedoed and sunk off the coast of Ireland.

Petrol rationing was introduced throughout Britain on 24 September and on the last day of the month, identity cards were issued.

To a large extent life went on as normal in Southampton. On 2 October, Sidney Miller of Richmond Road, a milk roundsman by trade, was summoned to appear before the magistrates for not having proper control of his horse in Coventry Road.

The prosecuting solicitor, Mr Noel Scragg, explained that on 11 September, Miller was delivering milk but he had walked some distance from his horse and cart and when he returned, they had gone. Constable W.H. Baker was on duty in Hill Lane, close to the junction with Howard Road, when he saw the horse, with the cart still attached, galloping towards him.

Bravely, Constable Baker stepped into the road, stopped all the other traffic and tried to stop the horse which then swerved towards the right. Baker managed to grab the reins but his arm was twisted and he was dragged into the side of the cart where he was struck by several milk bottles. Eventually, though, he did manage to stop the horse, but the officer did have to go to hospital later to have his injuries treated. The magistrates decided to fine Miller 20*s*. and commended Constable Baker for his actions.

On 3 October, British forces moved to the Belgian border, expecting an invasion at that point. By the 11th of the month there were about 140,000 British troops in France.

On 12 October, a young boy aged just 11 appeared before the magistrates at Southampton. He was charged with twenty-two separate offences including twelve of housebreaking, two of attempted housebreaking, five of larceny and three of malicious damage. The court heard that in sixteen of these cases he had acted alone, but in the remainder he had an accomplice, another boy who was just 10 years old.

On one occasion, the boy had knocked on the door of a house in Juniper Road, Bitterne, and asked for a drink of water. The householder could not help but notice that the boy had two live chickens under his coat and the police were called.

Details were given about the damage caused by the boy when he had broken into houses. He had not just stolen things but he had also smashed panes of glass, smeared paint on furniture and upset pots of jam onto carpets and other surfaces. In one case he had even damaged a gas meter, causing gas to leak into the house. Fortunately, when the homeowner came back he spotted the damage immediately and the gas leak was repaired before any naked flames were lit.

However, this was not the first time the boy had appeared in court. The previous year he had been bound over for twelve months after stealing cigarettes. As a result of that the court decided that he should be sent to an approved school for such a period as the authorities might see fit.

His young accomplice was also in court, charged with four cases of breaking and entering, one case of breaking with intent, one case of larceny and one of damaging the gas meter. The court decided to place the younger boy on probation for a year and he would be required to repay 9d. per week out of his 1s. pocket money until the sum of £1 had been recovered.

A terrible event took place on 14 October, which brought the reality of war home to so many British families including some living in Southampton. It was on that date that HMS *Royal Oak*, a veteran of the Battle of Jutland in the First World War, had been sunk in Scapa Flow. She had been at anchor when *U47* fired three torpedoes, one of which struck the ship in the bow. Of the ship's complement of 1,234 men and boys, a total of 833 were killed.

Over the next week, the details of some of those casualties were published in the local newspapers. Amongst the early reports were detailed the deaths of George Alexander McMillan, a teenager of Firgrove Road. Mark Warren Stephens, who acted as a cook on the ship and who had lived in Ascupart Street, was also lost. However, Sub Lieutenant Jeffrey Vincent of the Royal Marines and who lived in Gordon Avenue was amongst the survivors.

A few days later, a number of other casualties were listed. These included Alan Jack Clark who was only 18 and had lived in Priory Road with his parents. He had been a keen artist before the war and won a scholarship to Southampton Art School. He had had ambitions of becoming a signwriter but at the age of 15 had chosen instead to join the Royal Navy. He had only been posted to the *Royal Oak* in June.

A case of attempted murder was heard by the magistrates on 18 October. Percy Harold Lock, a labourer from Compton Walk, was charged with the attempted murder of Laura Violet Winifred Cobb, aged 19, a machinist from Paget Street. It was alleged that on

27 August, after a brief argument, Lock had gone up to Laura in the street and stabbed her several times with a knife he had once used for cutting cabbages.

Whilst she was giving evidence, Laura produced a leather handbag which had several holes where the knife had penetrated as she used it to defend herself. She was, however, still injured a number of times and at one stage the knife was sticking out of her head. She screamed and her assailant then ran away shouting, 'What have I done?' She pulled the knife out of her head and threw it to one side before knocking on a door nearby and asking for help.

Maria Lock, the mother of the accused man, told the court that her son was a widower and had lived with her for some time. She had only known of the relationship between Percy and Laura for a month before the attack. On the Sunday before the attack, Percy had told his mother that he had arranged to meet Miss Cobb at the pier but on the day she did not turn up. The next Sunday was 27 August and this time he had arranged to take Laura for a ride on his motorcycle but again she did not appear. Percy then mentioned that he and Laura were going to meet later in the Newcastle public house. At 10.00pm, Percy had arrived home and said he and Laura had had an argument because he had seen her walk into the Newcastle with another man. Percy then went out again.

Edward George Hurst testified that he had been walking down James Street when he heard shouting. There was a girl lying on the pavement and a man standing over her. The man appeared to be punching her.

Inspector Chambers told the court that at around 11.00pm, the accused had walked into the police station and said: 'I have come to give myself up. I have just stabbed a woman.'

Giving evidence on his own behalf, Lock explained that he had seen Miss Cobb in the Newcastle with another man and words passed between them. He then went home, told his mother that he had argued with his girl, collected his sheath knife and went back to the same pub. Later, Miss Cobb came in again and she was still with the other man but he left almost immediately. Lock followed Miss Cobb out and they argued in the street. He asked that they put all the arguments behind them but she said that she did not want to see him again. He then took out the knife and stabbed her in the back. After that he seemed to go wild and didn't come to his senses until he saw her lying on the ground, screaming.

Having heard all the testimony, the magistrates sent Lock for trial at the next assizes at Winchester. That trial took place on 29 November before Mr Justice Croom-Johnson. Lock now faced two charges, one of attempted murder and one of wounding with intent to cause grievous bodily harm. He initially pleaded not guilty to both but once he had heard some of the prosecution evidence, he asked to plead guilty to the lesser charge of wounding. That plea was accepted and Lock received a sentence of twelve months' imprisonment.

In the first week of November there were reports of two separate accidents in Southampton, where men had died after falling into air-raid shelters, during the blackout.

The second of these was 64-year-old Patrick Crawley of 70 Lime Street who had suffered a fractured skull when he fell into a shelter on the night of 7 November. The shelter was one of several enclosed by blocks of flats in Lime Street and King Street. The accident had apparently taken place whilst Patrick was walking home at about 7.00pm but it was only discovered when he staggered into his home at 8.00pm, looking pale and ill. The doctor was called and he was taken to hospital but died from his injuries the following morning.

Just one week before this, 40-year-old Lily Bond of Wilton Crescent had also perished when she fell down the steps of a shelter in Regent's Park. Mrs Bond was an Air Raid Precautions (ARP) driver and had gone to the shelter to meet her husband, Bertie. She was walking towards her husband's car when she fell into the shelter.

Another tragedy unfolded on 11 November, this time at the South Western Hotel. Captain Reginald Oliver, a military railway transport officer from Ealing in London, had used his service revolver to take his own life, leaving a letter on the mantelpiece of the fireplace inside his room. Attached to the letter was a £1 note with a message saying that it was for the chambermaid who, presumably, Captain Oliver had assumed would find his body. In fact, the discovery was made by a fellow officer who had gone to the room on the second floor to see Captain Oliver. He had seen a bullet case in the corridor outside the room and a hole in the door. Looking through that hole he could clearly see the captain's body on the bed, the revolver in his right hand.

The hotel manager was called and he used his key to gain admittance to the room. It was believed that the first shot had been fired whilst Captain Oliver was leaning over the wash basin, as blood was found there. It was this shot which caused the hole in the door and afterwards, the captain had lain on the bed and fired the second shot into his head. It had ricocheted around the room and finished up on the carpet at the foot of the bed.

It was reported that Captain Oliver had recently been involved in a minor road accident when he was struck by a vehicle, sustaining slight injuries to his leg. He was a widower with a young daughter but had been very depressed of late. An inquest would duly return a verdict of suicide.

ARP worker John Clarke appeared in police court on 15 November charged with being drunk and disorderly and assaulting Constable Victor White whilst in the execution of his duty on 10 November.

White had encountered Clarke after the latter had been ejected from a public house in the High Street at 8.45pm. He heard Clarke shouting and went over to him to tell him to be quiet. Clarke continued shouting and claimed that someone had stolen his wallet and money inside it. When asked his name Clarke told the officer not to bother himself and was advised to go home.

A quarter of an hour later Constable White saw Clarke again in the same place. When approached this time, Clarke said that he had had his hat and coat stolen. White suggested that he might have left them in the pub.

Later still that same night the constable heard Clarke shouting for the police yet again. He found Clarke lying on his back at the entrance to an air-raid shelter. He was kicking his legs and struck White when he approached. Clarke was so violent White had to handcuff him and take him to the police station.

In court, Clarke claimed that he had no memory of assaulting Constable White. He added that it was his first night off from ARP duties in two months, and that he had been working night and day. The assault charge was dismissed, but Clarke was fined £1.15s. costs for being drunk and disorderly.

On 24 November, a terrible accident took place in New Road. Mrs MacLennan of Sunnyside Cottages, Cedar Road, was walking along New Road, heading towards the Civic Centre. Her 3-year-old daughter, Marylin Joan, was on the opposite side of the road, with her aunt, who was pushing a pram holding Marylin's baby sister.

Suddenly, Marylin ran into the road, towards her mother. At that precise moment a corporation bus was approaching and the child stepped directly in front of it. The driver swerved but he couldn't avoid hitting Marylin whose body rolled underneath the bus in full view of her mother and aunt. An ambulance was called but before it could arrive, a taxi driver took the injured girl to the hospital. It was there that it was discovered that the child was already dead, having suffered a fractured skull and a broken left arm and leg.

The month of December began with the announcement that conscription had been increased to include men aged between 19 and 41. There was, however, some good news on the war front. The Battle of the River Plate had taken place on the 13th, causing the *Graf Spee* to retreat into Montevideo harbour after being attacked by HMS *Exeter*, HMS *Ajax* and the *Achilles*. The ship was forced to leave the safety of the harbour on 17 December and was scuttled by its captain, Hans Langsdorff.

In the same month, the first Canadian troops arrived in Britain, to be followed, about a week later, by the first Indian troops. However, towards the end of the month, meat rationing was introduced, something that was expected but not welcomed.

An inquest opened on 5 December into the deaths of a devoted married couple, 54-year-old Ernest Henry Lynch and his 55-year-old wife Edith Georgina, who had lived together in Foundry Lane. They had been found dead on 24 November and the cause of their deaths was coal-gas poisoning.

Ernest had been unemployed for some six weeks prior to his death, but that wasn't their main concern for Edith had been suffering from mental health problems for more than three years and of late had grown steadily worse. This had culminated in June 1939, when she had tried to kill herself by putting her head in the gas oven. For that she was committed to Knowle Mental Hospital as a voluntary patient. Despite receiving medical attention, Edith's condition did not improve and Ernest, it seemed, had decided on drastic action.

Ethel Williams was Ernest's sister-in-law and she told the inquest that on 22 November, Ernest had told her that he couldn't come to her house for tea the following day, as arranged, as he had let some rooms at his home and the people were moving in then. Ethel believed him but called at Ernest's house two days later, on 24 November. She got no reply to her knocking and upon returning home told her husband that she was worried that something bad had happened. Her husband went and reported the matter to the police and Sergeant William Moore forced an entry to the house at 8.00pm that same evening. He found the bodies of Ernest and Edith lying side by side on the bed. Their cat, also dead, lay on the floor.

Ernest had left a note behind, explaining exactly what he had done. It was addressed to Ethel Williams and read:

Dear Doll,

No doubt you will be horrified at what I have done before you read this, but believe me there was no other way of solving our problems.

In spite of the kindness of doctors and staff at Knowle, Edie is not a bit better than she was when she made the attempt to end her agony in June. So, on Sunday last I promised to bring her back and help her out, and I have no compunction in doing so.

The only thing I am sorry for is that I can't survive her long enough to have her cremated, as she always wished me to do.

It is her wish and mine that you shall have everything we have, as some small recompense for your kindness at all times.

I hope you will not have the unpleasant task of finding us, but I can't see any way of assuring myself that someone else will.

Try and forgive me if I have caused you any sorrow, but honestly it will be better for Edie and I have no intention of living without her; life would be too empty.

As expected, the decision at the inquest was that Ernest had murdered his wife and then taken his own life.

On the penultimate day of the year, Corporal Bernard Winchester arrived home at his bungalow in Bitterne, on belated Christmas leave and had only been home a few hours when he was awakened by his wife to find the bungalow on fire. Fortunately, the door to his 6-month-old son Colin's bedroom had been shut, but the paint on the door was blistered by the heat.

The Winchesters had gone to bed at 11.00pm but Mrs Winchester woke at about 2.30am to find the bedroom full of smoke. At first she thought it was just fog but soon she came to realise that it was smoke. Having woken her husband, they wrapped Colin in a blanket and escaped from the house. Corporal Winchester tried to enter the drawing room, but was beaten back by heat and flames. They roused the neighbours and Woolston fire brigade was called. Two engines were sent and they managed to confine the fire to the front room, but most of the furniture was destroyed and, sadly, it was not insured. A large hole was burned in the floor and clothing and items in other rooms were discoloured by the smoke. Corporal Winchester's uniform was destroyed, but firemen were able to save his wallet containing his holiday money.

The year 1939 had opened with many people afraid that the UK might be dragged into another major war with Germany. It ended with the knowledge that their worst fears had been realised and this time there were no suggestions that it would be a short affair. The country as a whole knew that this would be a long and bloody conflict.

CHAPTER TWO

1940

In early January it was revealed that eighty Poles, including twenty women, stranded in Southampton and unable to speak a word of English had gone back to school, in the classrooms of the former girl's grammar school, to learn the language. They were passengers on the vessel *Chobry*, which had left Poland on her maiden voyage to South America in July 1939. Just before she was due to return to her home country, war had broken out and she was now without a home port as that had fallen into the hands of the Germans. The vessel had sailed for Southampton and, though she had now left, some of the crew had stayed behind.

The Polish Consul, Mr Komierowski, had then got in touch with the local education centre which had initially set up a social centre in the school, but this had then developed into an educational centre and volunteer tutors were now teaching the men and women English. None of the tutors spoke Polish but they were fluent in French and German and many of the pupils also understood those languages.

Other classes were also taught including basket making, art, woodwork and other crafts. Apparently progress was very rapid and the teachers described their pupils as the most eager they had ever taught. A few days after the report of the Polish classes appeared, the newspapers carried a report stating that basic foodstuffs were going to be rationed.

Rationing began to bite in January. On the 8th, food rationing was introduced, and it was clear by now that the war would be a long, drawn-out affair and most believed that more items would be in short supply in the future.

Another inquiry into a mysterious death took place on 19 January. This time the individual who had perished was 46-year-old Charles Henry Belbin, an engraver by trade.

Mr Belbin was a native of Beckenham in Kent and had a wife and young family there. At the outbreak of war, he had unfortunately lost

The preparation of defences, in case invasion came.

his job and been forced to seek alternative employment. After some searching he had found a position at the Ordnance Survey in South-ampton and had travelled to the town on 30 September 1939 and taken lodgings at 8 Havelock Road, where his landlady was Emma Charlotte Williams.

From the outset Emma saw that Charles was morose, quiet and depressed. He missed his family a great deal and did not see them again, apart from a short visit over the Christmas period. That had been a very pleasant time but it was a most unhappy Charles who returned to Southampton in the New Year.

On 13 January, Emma left home at 5.45pm in order to go to the theatre. At the time, Charles was sitting in the kitchen reading a newspaper. When she returned at about 8.00pm she found her lodger in a crumpled heap at the foot of the stairs and could not wake him. The ambulance and police were called but Charles was beyond all aid.

At first Emma assumed that this had been a terrible accident and Charles had fallen down the stairs and been killed but when the body was moved by the ambulance men, a small empty brown glass bottle was found underneath Charles.

Charles's room was then searched by the police and two pieces of evidence were discovered which appeared to throw light upon the

Some of Southampton's evacuated children on their way to safety in the country, early January 1940.

matter. The first was a note on a writing pad. Dated 15 December, it was in Charles's handwriting and read, 'I have lost my wife, my children, my good name, my house and home, my job and my mind, so one day I shall end it all.'

The other was a pencilled note on the back of a letter from Charles's wife. It simply read, 'Well goodbye all; this is the end.'

At the inquest it was revealed that although Charles was certainly depressed and had, in two penned messages, intimated that he might take his own life, the brown bottle would need to be examined before a verdict could be reached. The bottle was handed over to the Borough Analyst, Mr Sidney Emsley, who found that it had contained aconite.

In his summing up, the coroner commented that despite the fact that there had been poison in the bottle and in Charles's stomach contents there was no actual proof that he had taken his own life. There were two notes but one was dated some time previously and the other was undated. In the circumstances, the verdict was that Charles had died from aconite poisoning in circumstances unknown.

Two days after the inquest into the death of Charles, the news broke that HMS *Exmouth* had been torpedoed by a German U-boat. Every member of its 135 crew was lost and this included souls from Southampton.

The people of Southampton were incensed to find, as they walked to work on the morning of Friday, 16 February, that two monuments had been defaced during the previous night.

Red paint had been poured over both the *Titanic* memorial and the statue of Palmerston. The vandalism was presumed to be the work of an anti-war organisation and the police believed that more than one individual must have been responsible.

One tin of paint had been poured over the head of the bronze figure on the *Titanic* memorial and this had run down over the inscription dedicated to those who gave their lives to save other passengers. Another tin of paint had been emptied over the head of the statue of Palmerston and this had run down the length of the entire figure. An initial attempt was made to clean the statue on the Friday morning but workmen discovered that the paint had already eaten into the stonework and restoration would be a major job. Samples of the paint were collected for analysis in the hope that the manufacturer might be traced which would in turn lead to the identification of

The statue of Palmerston, attacked by vandals who daubed it with paint in March 1940.

retailers who sold that paint who might be able to supply a list of customers.

As these efforts progressed passers-by made their own comments on the vandalism with one man stating, 'It's a pity they didn't break their necks while they were doing it', another adding, 'Tarring and feathering would be too good for them.'

On 11 March, meat rationing began in Britain. This had been introduced earlier, as mentioned in the previous chapter, but now it became reality.

There was some good news for the travelling populace on the next day, 12 March. The corporation announced that from now on both tram and bus services were to be extended. Trams would return to their pre-war timetables meaning that the last tram would run 30 minutes later. These trams would now leave the town centre for the various terminals at 11.00pm instead of 10.30pm.

Bus services too would be extended with the last ones leaving the town centre at 10.45pm. However, the authorities advised the general public not to wait for the last vehicles as these would be very crowded and only a finite number of passengers could be accommodated.

Three days later, in the early hours of 15 March, the blackout in Southampton claimed another victim when 'George', the town's oldest traffic light situated at the junction of Hill Lane, Archer's Road and Howard Road, was knocked over by an ambulance.

The vehicle had been driven by Albert Monk of 1 Manchester Street and he had two men with him, Leslie Hines and William Hurst. The latter received a fractured wrist in the accident whilst the other two men needed treatment for cuts and bruises. 'George' was not as fortunate and had to be removed. A policeman on point-duty replaced him.

On 27 March, the story of a soldier on leave from France gladdened people's hearts. John Canny was home on leave and enjoying time with his wife and children at their home in Dock Street. His third child, a 7-year-old daughter named Kathleen, was standing in front of the fire in the parlour when her dress suddenly caught fire. Quick as a flash, John leapt to his feet and beat out the flames with his hands, suffering burns in the process. The little girl also received superficial burns to her back and legs but it could have been so much worse had her father not been there. She recovered in hospital.

At the end of the month, on 28 March to be precise, the UK and France made a formal agreement that neither country would seek to

The destruction of 'George', the town's oldest traffic light, in March 1940.

Staff at Southampton's ARP Headquarters getting used to wearing their respirators at work.

make a separate peace with Germany. Two days later, on the 30th, police were investigating a mystery death at 50 Malmesbury Road, Shirley. Upon going into the house, officers found the body of 69-year-old Frederick Mason Candy in the corner of a bedroom.

It was clear that Mr Candy had been dead for several hours but the cause was uncertain. There was some blood on the floor but no signs of violence apart from a few minor scratches which appeared to be self-inflicted. The dead man lay propped against the wall with his head thrown back.

The body had originally been found by the dead man's brother, Stanley Harold Candy, who also lived in the house. Stanley had gone to his brother's bedroom at 8.30am, and found that Frederick was dead. Stanley had last seen his brother alive at 10.30pm the previous night. At that time Frederick had said that he felt very cold and Stanley gave him an extra shirt, which he put on.

After finding his brother's body, Stanley went to the police station at Shirley to report the matter. Officers visited the house and called in the police surgeon, Dr Havers. He confirmed that Frederick was dead but was unable to immediately determine the cause of death.

In early April, a new Chief Constable, Mr H.C. Allen, was appointed to the Borough police force. His inauguration was attended by a large number of senior officers. Representatives of the council and the press were also in attendance.

The new Chief Constable, Mr H.C. Allen, with senior officers of the Borough Police Force.

On 8 April, an open verdict was returned at an inquest on Frank Grevett, 65, a master tailor of 38 London Road, Southampton, who had fallen from a second-floor window at his premises.

Maud Grevett, the widow of the dead man, told the court that she had last seen her husband alive on the afternoon of the tragedy. He seemed to be very bright and happy. She went on to say that three-and-a-half years ago her husband had had an operation to remove a cataract from his right eye. He was already blind in the other eye. As a result, he had been very depressed over the last few years and suffered a lot from dizziness, especially if he bent over. He had financial concerns and was also worried because she had asked him for a divorce and he had refused. On 3 April he had told her that he felt he would have to close down the business and if he did so, he would not have enough money to maintain her and their 12-year-old son. He had, on a previous occasion, threatened to put his head in the gas oven.

Frederick William Birmingham had worked for Mr Grevett for the past four years and he described his employer as a very quiet and reserved man. He had last seen Mr Grevett alive at 7.00pm on Friday, 5 April. He was not aware of any of his employer's troubles.

Ronald Henry Winteridge, a meat trader of 36 London Road, testified that he had found Mr Grevett lying unconscious in the rear yard of No. 38 at 7.45pm on the 5th. The sound of groaning coming from the yard had attracted Mr Winteridge's attention. Mr Grevett was rushed to hospital but died soon afterwards.

Constable John Furlong testified that the window Mr Grevett had fallen through was 32ft from the ground. The window was open 18in and, in his opinion, it was highly unlikely that someone could simply have fallen from that point. The coroner recorded that Mr Grevett had died from injuries received by falling from the window in circumstances unknown.

In Europe, at the same time, a new theatre of war opened and this time it was Norway. On 9 April, German troops landed in several Norwegian ports and captured the capital Oslo. Allied soldiers were quick to respond. British and French forces landed north of Trondheim and, on the following day, close to Narvik. The struggle for the country lasted until the end of the month when the Allied forces withdrew.

A tragic story of a young boy's death was told at an inquest in mid-April. The victim in this case was 11-year-old Dennis Ivan Lawes of Pine Grove Road, Sholing.

Dennis's mother was a little angry with her son. At some time between 6.00pm and 6.15pm the boy was getting ready to go out and play with his friends when his mother noticed that there was sand on his shoes. This meant that he had been playing in a large sandpit at a builder's merchants in Station Road and she had told him more than once that it was dangerous and he wasn't allowed to play there. Dennis promised that he wouldn't go back to the sandpit and then ran outside.

Moments later he had met three of his friends. Jack Malcolm Barnes was the eldest at 13 and with him were Ronald John Stone, aged 11, and Cyril Victor Wheedon, who was 12. The four boys immediately went to the sandpit and began to play.

The game was a simple one. The boys would climb up the sand and then jump off. They played this for some 15 minutes or so and then Dennis and Cyril stayed at the bottom digging holes whilst the other two sat at the top.

Suddenly there was a fall of sand and Dennis found himself trapped by the leg. He found this highly amusing, laughed heartily and wouldn't allow Cyril to help him escape. Soon, though, Dennis discovered that the sand was packed too tightly for him to get his leg out. He was still trying to do so when a second fall buried him completely. Later estimates would put the total sand covering the boy at somewhere between 15 and 20 tons.

The boys made a valiant attempt to rescue their friend, using their bare hands and they were helped by some passers-by. By the time they found Dennis he was dead, the cause being asphyxiation.

Meanwhile, on 17 April another inquest opened, this time for 58-year-old Catherine Gelling who had been found dead in her bed in New Road the previous Sunday.

Emily May Tracey, who also lived in New Road and acted as a cleaner for the deceased woman, explained to the court that she had only known Mrs Gelling for three months but during that time had seen that she was a very heavy drinker and had a particular fondness for stout and ale. So bad had her drinking become that recently she had been attended by a doctor who ordered her to be admitted to hospital. Within a day or so, however, Mrs Gelling had discharged herself and returned home.

In the week before her death, Mrs Gelling had asked Emily to fetch her some drink but she had refused, hoping that the absence of alcohol might improve Mrs Gelling's health. On 10 April, though,

Emily noticed a bottle at the side of the bed and this contained methylated spirit, olive oil and ground ginger. To be on the safe side, Emily removed the bottle and placed it on a high shelf, out of reach, where it remained for a few days but, on the day Mrs Gelling's body was discovered, Emily saw that the bottle had been taken down and most of the contents had been drained. There was a cup on a table by the bed and this had clearly held some of the rather foul liquid. The coroner returned an open verdict.

On 9 May, conscription in Britain was extended. The very next day, Germany invaded Belgium, France, Luxembourg and the Netherlands. There had been much debate in the House of Commons over the government's handling of the Norwegian invasion and the Prime Minister had been heavily criticised. His position now became untenable and on 10 May, he tendered his resignation. He was replaced by Winston Churchill, who was called upon to form a war-time coalition government.

There was yet another invasion on the 10th but this time it was the UK invading Iceland, fearful that otherwise the Germans would target the island and use it as a military base to attack the north.

On the same day that all this was happening across Europe, an inquest opened in Southampton into the death of 20-year-old cyclist Aubrey Thomas Harris who had received fatal injuries in a collision with a motor car in Glebe Road.

Ernest Walter Harris, the father of the dead man, explained to the court that his son was rather short-sighted and needed to wear glasses and this may well have contributed to his death.

Two men who were cycling with the deceased, Leslie Harris, the brother of the dead man, and Stanley Milne, testified that they were all riding in single file and turned from Anglesea Terrace into Glebe Road. The boys saw a car approaching and it seemed to be crossing the road. Milne, who was at the front of the group, stopped and Aubrey had to swerve to avoid him, which brought him into the path of the car. Milne stated that he did not think the driver of the car was in any way to blame for the accident.

For his part, the driver, Ronald Charles Baden Harbut, said that two cats ran out of some shrubbery and he had to swerve to avoid them. He also stated that the cyclists all appeared to be riding very fast. Having heard the testimony of the witnesses, a verdict of death by misadventure was returned.

On 11 May, the Germans occupied Luxembourg. It was clear that Germany was making great advances all along the front and it was two days later, on 13 May, that the new Prime Minister, Winston Churchill, made his famous speech in the House of Commons, stating that he had nothing to offer but blood, toil, tears and sweat. The very next day the Local Defence Volunteers, later renamed the Home Guard, was formed by the new Secretary of State for War, Anthony Eden.

British and French forces were being pushed back to the coast and many were trapped around Dunkirk. Fortunately, Hitler ordered the advance to stop and decided to allow the Luftwaffe to attack the thousands of men trapped on and around the beaches. A marvellous plan was hatched to evacuate as many as possible by using a flotilla of ships of all sizes from the southern coast of England. The operation began on 26 May and by the time the operation was completed in early June over 300,000 men had been saved.

On the very same day that the evacuation from Dunkirk began, Southampton introduced 'Anti-Gossip Week'. This was an attempt to bring home to the populace the danger of idle gossip. Banners were hung across the streets and the docks. One, at the entrance to No. 2 Dock gate, read, 'Did YOU sink that ship by idle gossip'. Another method of educating people was the little white cards that people heard making dangerous gossip might well find gently pushed into their hands. On the front of the card was printed 'With the compliments of the Voluntary Information Committee' whilst on the back was 'Don't you think gossip might be dangerous?'. A thousand of these cards had been printed and would be handed out by members of the committee.

There can be no doubt that the evacuation of children from the major towns and cities saved many young lives during the war but two separate stories at the end of May 1940 illustrated that it could also lead to tragedy for both involved the deaths of Southampton children.

Thelma Kettle, who was just 10 years old, lived with her parents at 13 Bromley Road, Bitterne Park but had been evacuated to Lymington where she was billeted with the Arnold family. By all accounts, Thelma was very happy with them and was treated as one of their own.

The eldest son of the house was 26-year-old Joseph Leonard Arnold and he decided to go out onto the river, in a rowing boat, to pick up

One of the banners for anti-gossip week in May 1940.

some fishing lines. He asked Thelma if she would like to go with him and she excitedly agreed. As they sailed along they approached a pier where another boat was moored and this was drifting out into the river. Joseph's boat was close to it and he said it would have to be pushed away gently. As he leaned over the side to do so, Thelma decided she would help and stood up in the boat. As she approached the side of the rowing boat it overbalanced, casting Thelma and Joseph into the water.

Joseph swam around for some time trying to find Thelma but without success. This particular tragedy did not, however, end there for the following day Joseph, deeply remorseful, told his family he was going out the back to mend his bicycle. Instead of doing so he took his father's gun from the shed, walked to a public convenience in a nearby park and shot himself.

The other incident involved 11-year-old Phyllis Roe, the adopted daughter of Mr and Mrs Frederick Limburn of 3 Radstock Road in Southampton. She too had been evacuated to the country and in her case was placed with the Scadding family of Parkstone in Dorset.

On the day in question Phyllis had said she wanted a bath. Mrs Gwendoline Scadding lit the copper in the bathroom but after a few minutes the gas went out. Being careful to turn the tap off first, Gwendoline then went out to do some shopping. She claimed that she was only out of the house 5 minutes or so when her eldest son ran up to her and said he thought there was something wrong as he couldn't get any reply from Phyllis who had locked herself in the bathroom.

Running home quickly, Gwendoline had to climb into the bathroom through the window and upon gaining access found Phyllis lying in the bathwater, her head leaning against the wall but out of the water. There was no smell of gas and Mrs Scadding couldn't get a light until she put more money in the meter.

At the inquest Frederick Cole from the gas company said that he had made an examination of the equipment and found a bad leak in the rubber tubing that ran into the copper boiler.

It can be said that it had been evacuation that led to two little girls from Southampton and a young man from Lymington losing their lives.

An inquiry into the death of Sergeant Major Arthur Devereux Rice Adams was concluded at an inquest at Netley Hospital on Wednesday, 29 May.

On the previous Sunday, 26 May, Private Harry Hughes had been on sentry duty at Southampton docks. It was 2.50am when he heard a car approaching at approximately 30mph. Hughes gave the usual challenge, 'Halt, who goes there?' but the vehicle did not even slow down, let alone stop. The second challenge, 'Halt or I'll shoot', was then given but still the car did not slow down. Hughes fired one shot, aiming at the left rear tyre and then the car slowed and came to a standstill. Going to investigate, Hughes found that Adams, who was a front-seat passenger, had been hit.

Some citizens went that extra step with their bomb shelters. This lady turned hers into a garden feature.

Adams was rushed to Netley Hospital where he was treated by Dr John Myles Mitchell. After examining his patient, Dr Mitchell determined that he had been shot in the back on the left side, close to his spine. As a result, Adams was now paralysed from the waist down and had other internal injuries. Despite medical treatment, Adams died that afternoon and a subsequent post-mortem revealed fragments of metal in his body which were consistent with the bullet having passed through the back of the car and the car seat.

Private Hughes had, of course, merely been doing his duty and there were two witnesses who testified that he had acted correctly and issued the two required warnings before firing his rifle. The first of these was Lance Corporal William Millington who was the guard commander at the sentry post. The other witness was Major Harold Dunmore Lane of the RAMC who had been nearby at the time.

Private William Green was the driver of the car and he claimed that he had not seen the sentry or heard the two challenges. The first he knew of anything was when he heard a shot and saw his passenger slump forward in his seat.

Having heard all the witnesses, the coroner stated that no blame could be attached to Private Hughes and the inquest concluded that this was a case of death by misadventure.

Sergeant Major Adams left six daughters, two of whom were in court to hear all the evidence and who, after it was over, sought out Private Hughes and shook his hand, pointing out that he was only doing his duty and should feel no guilt. It was a doubly sad time for those six daughters, for only seven weeks prior to this tragedy, they had lost their mother too.

On 10 June Italy finally declared war on France and the UK. On the same day Norway surrendered to the Germans. On the very next day, 11 June, the *Southampton Echo* reported a horrific event. It was a story told by Thomas McCarthy Hamilton, a 32-year-old chief petty officer who lived at 18 Gainsford Road.

Hamilton had been serving on the SS *Abukir*, which had been torpedoed and sunk in the North Sea whilst evacuating British and Belgian soldiers, airmen and civilians from Ostend.

Sergeant Major Adams who was shot after his car failed to stop at a sentry post at the docks in May 1940.

As the ship slowly headed for England, the Luftwaffe attacked for almost 90 minutes, but failed to hit her. Then, however, in the early hours of 28 May, an E-boat began to attack. The *Abukir* took a zig-zag course and managed to avoid two torpedoes. Two more were then fired. The first one missed but the final one struck amidships, cutting the *Abukir* in two. She sank within a minute but it was what happened next that formed the basis of Hamilton's story.

The ship sank within a minute but Hamilton survived and swam away from her. To his horror he watched as the E-boat put out strong searchlights and began spraying the survivors with machine guns. Hamilton related how the chief officer was clinging to some wreckage a few feet away from him. He was hit in the head and slowly slid beneath the waves. Only some 20 people survived the sinking out of a total of 241 people on board.

Meanwhile, three days later in Southampton, on the 14th, the funeral took place of Leading Aircraftman Arthur Lewis, the only son of Mr and Mrs Lewis of Church House, Cross Street, who was killed on active service. Arthur had joined the RAF just over two years previously and had served as a wireless instructor and operator. He had recently been recommended for a commission.

It was also in June that another inquest heard of the tragic death of 8-year-old Brian Reginald Lampard, an evacuee, whose parents resided in Itchen. Brian had gone for a walk with four other boys, one of whom was 12-year-old James Aston Hazelton. At one stage they walked over a railway footbridge but once they had passed, Brian had gone back. One of the younger boys suddenly cried out, 'He is killed', and when James looked back he saw Brian fall from the bridge onto the railway line. The injured boy was rushed to hospital but died there, from a fractured skull. The coroner recorded a verdict of accidental death and pointed out that it was impossible to fall from the bridge if it was used properly.

Though the newspapers of the time suppressed the information, the largest single loss of British life in a single event during the war took place on 17 June. The vessel RMS *Lancastria* was evacuating troops and other nationals from Saint-Nazaire when she was attacked by the Luftwaffe and sunk. Over 4,000 lives were lost.

The new Chief Constable, Mr H.C. Allen, who had only been in office a matter of two months, was involved in a road accident on the evening of 25 June. There were two cars in a small convoy, heading for the Civic Centre. The Chief Constable was in the first vehicle, which was driven by Constable Frank Muddiman. The second car held the Borough Engineer, Mr S.C. Stanton.

Whilst the two cars were travelling along The Avenue, Mr Allen saw someone show a light. This was, of course, during the blackout and seeing this Mr Allen ordered his driver to stop immediately. Constable Muddiman did as his commanding officer said and slammed on the brakes. He was just in the process of opening the driver's door to get out when the second car slammed into the back of the stationary vehicle.

The second car hit the Chief Constable's car in the offside rear and forced it forwards, into a tree, which it hit with some force. Mr Allen was thrown forward and sustained cuts to both of his hands, bruised ribs and an injured ankle. His driver got off lightly as he was wearing his gas-mask pack on his chest at the time and though he was thrown against the steering wheel, the pack took much of the force and Constable Muddiman escaped with a slightly bruised chest. As for Mr Stanton, he and his driver only received minor injuries.

The Chief Constable's car after the accident in The Avenue on 25 June 1940.

Mr Allen was taken to the hospital for a precautionary x-ray but the Borough Engineer was able to go on his way and attend the function at the Civic Hall. As for the individual who shone the light, caused the first car to stop and the other to ram into it, he was never found.

On the same day that the Chief Constable was making headlines in Southampton, France officially surrendered to Germany leaving the UK and the countries of the Empire to fight on alone. Three days later the Channel Islands were bombed. In Guernsey, thirty-three people were killed and sixty-seven injured, in Jersey, nine were killed and many injured. On the final day of June, German troops invaded the islands.

As the new month dawned on 1 July, the Channel Islands surrendered to the German forces and Hitler ordered plans to be drawn up for the invasion of mainland Britain. This was codenamed Operation Sealion but, in order to carry out his plans, Hitler would first of all have to gain air superiority over the RAF.

On 4 July, Sydney Fulford of 57 Northbrook Road told the local press of his lucky escape from the *Arandora Star*. This ship was originally a passenger liner of the Blue Star Line, which had been requisitioned as a troop ship at the outbreak of hostilities. At the end of June, she had been given the task of transporting German and Italian prisoners to Canada. These prisoners had been taken on board in Liverpool but early in the journey across the Atlantic she had been attacked by the submarine *U47*.

Sydney, who was a barman on board the ship, explained that his shipmates always called him 'Lucky' and the name seemed to be apt. Some weeks before he had been one of the last men to leave the *Narvik* and after joining the *Arandora Star* had a cabin close to the part of the ship struck by the torpedo. There had been a terrific explosion and the cabin was immediately plunged into darkness. Part of the deck had gone and when Sydney put his leg out of the bunk, there was nothing to support it. He was also covered in oil from a burst pipe.

Somehow, he and a fellow sailor managed to find the gangway but by the time they reached the deck, most of the lifeboats had gone. Many of them had been taken by Italian and German prisoners and Sydney saw British soldiers keeping more of the prisoners at bay with fixed bayonets.

Sydney finally managed to find a lifeboat and by that time the ship was low in the water. He then turned to watch the ship go down and saw many men still standing on the decks, not knowing what to do. He said that most of them would have had no chance of survival. In fact, 805 men had perished when the *Arandora Star* was attacked, most of them prisoners of war who had been too afraid to leave the sinking ship.

It was the same day, 4 July, when Sark became the last of the Channel Islands to surrender to the German forces. Five days later, on 9 July, the Battle of Britain began with the initial Luftwaffe attacks targeting shipping in the Channel. On the same day, Elizabeth Black, the owner of the Cadora Cafe in Bernard Street, appeared before the magistrates charged with selling intoxicating liquors without a licence.

Inspector Chambers explained to the court that he had gone to the cafe with two other officers at 3.20am on 17 April. Mrs Black was standing behind the counter. There were four other men in the cafe. Two of them, a sailor and a civilian, were sitting at a table with glasses of beer in front of them. The other two men were in conversation near a fireplace and there were glasses of beer on the mantelpiece near them. Behind the counter, in clear view, was a crate full of beer bottles which largely negated Mrs Black's immediate comment of, 'You can't stop them bringing it in. They brought it in themselves.'

The four men inside the cafe all confirmed Mrs Black's story but upon searching the premises Inspector Chambers and his men found 67 full half-pint bottles of beer and over 200 empty bottles. Mrs Black claimed that all these bottles, full or empty, belonged to her brother. However, when one of the police officers went upstairs to talk to Mrs Black's brother, he simply did not want to get involved and would confirm nothing.

Other witnesses were called for the defence and all claimed that they had taken their own beer into the cafe but the magistrates found the case proved and fined £25. She was given fourteen days to pay.

On the same day that Mrs Black appeared before the magistrates in Southampton, 19-year-old William Edward Spender appeared at the Hampshire assizes for holding up a cinema cashier with an imitation pistol.

Spender had been employed at the Classic Cinema in Southampton and he had seen the cashier making up the day's takings, a sum of £26.14s.4d. He then pointed the pistol at her and stole the money. He then tried to make good his getaway but was arrested at the railway station. Spender pleaded guilty in court and was sentenced to six months' imprisonment.

A sad story was outlined on 17 July when the newspapers told the story of 20-year-old Daisy Violet Whitcher of Birmingham Street.

Daisy, whose maiden name was Caplen, had married Walter Whitcher in early July, after which Walter, who was in the navy, had returned to his ship. That ship was subsequently involved in an action against a German vessel and during the attack, Walter had been badly injured, and later died from his wounds. When the ship returned home, Walter was buried with full military honours. He and Daisy had been married for just two weeks.

What could have been a very nasty accident indeed was narrowly avoided on 18 July. At about 7.30am Leonard Collins was driving his corporation bus towards Millbrook. Collins was travelling along Waterloo Road when, at the corner of Park Road, he saw, to his horror, a cyclist skid on the tramlines and fall directly in front of the bus. There was no way just applying the brakes would stop the bus in time so Leonard had to swerve into a tram standard.

A number of passengers were injured including Mrs Ivy Blaske of Oxford Avenue and Miss Dorothy West of Athelstan Road, Bitterne. Both ladies were taken to hospital but fortunately their injuries were relatively minor. The cyclist, Horace Robinson of Oakley Road, Shirley, was also given hospital treatment for an injured hand but the prompt reactions of Leonard Collins had prevented what could have been a major road accident.

Two serious cases were dealt with by the Recorder, Mr W. Blake Odgers, at Southampton quarter sessions on Wednesday, 24 July. The first of these was an appeal against a sentence of six months' imprisonment on a shopkeeper, Frederick Kirk, of Broadlands Road. He had been sentenced for purchasing regimental accessories and clothing from Trooper Robert Ball Palmer who was himself now due to appear at Derbyshire assizes.

It had all started rather slowly when Palmer had offered to sell an army blanket to Kirk who then asked if he might be able to get other items from the stores. Eventually, Kirk ended up purchasing fifty-two blankets, eighteen pairs of socks, fifteen shirts, twelve pullovers, two carving knives, sixteen other knives, thirteen spoons, fifty-two forks and other sundry items. Pointing out that this was disgraceful when the country was at war, Mr Odgers had no difficulty in dismissing the appeal.

The second case was that of 23-year-old Harold Sydney Hockey of no fixed abode. He pleaded guilty to breaking into a house in Bassett Avenue on 14 May and stealing two rings, three bracelets and other articles to the value of £39.19s. He had gained entry to the premises by making a hole in the kitchen window of the house, reaching in and unfastening the catch. Not the most able of housebreakers, Hockey had managed to leave his fingerprints behind and, since he had a long criminal record, the police had little trouble in identifying him. Hockey asked for eight other charges to be taken into consideration including robberies in Chandler's Ford and Winchester in addition to other cases in Southampton. He received a sentence of three years' imprisonment.

At the end of the month good news was received by two Southampton families, both of whom had sons who had been reported as missing in action. Both families were now informed that their sons were alive and were prisoners of war.

One of these was Corporal Edward James Freestone, the second son of a widow, Alice Freestone of Surrey Road, Woolston. Edward, who was 21, had been reported missing on 26 May. His brother, William, had been called up for military service just two days before Alice had heard that Edward was still alive.

The second prisoner of war was Private Alfred George Mason Poynter, whose parents resided in Romsey Road, Maybush. He had been seen on a beach at Boulogne just before his unit was picked up by a destroyer. Alfred had, for some reason, been unable to stay with his comrades and, consequently, had been reported missing in action. Alfred was one of three members of his family serving in the forces. His sister was in the Auxiliary Territorial Service and his younger brother was in the Merchant Navy. His parents were delighted to hear their son had been taken prisoner but was still alive and well.

On the first day of August Adolf Hitler set a date of 15 September for the invasion of mainland Britain. On the same day an inquest was held at Southampton before the Coroner, Mr Arthur Emanuel where it was detailed that a flapping canary had led to the discovery of the body of 43-year-old Rose Brown of 103 Northumberland Road.

Evidence of identification was given by Rose's husband, George, who stated that in their nine years of marriage his wife had always been in good health. Medical evidence was given by Dr J.P. Murphy, who had performed a post-mortem on the dead woman. He had noted a small white mark around Rose's neck, which might have been caused by the tightness of her clothing. It was possible that she had slipped on a highly polished floor and struck her throat on a nearby ottoman.

Agnes Wooldridge, who lived next door at No. 103, said that she saw that Mrs Brown's door was open. Agnes went to close the door because there were several cats around and she knew that Rose had a canary which the cats might have been after. As she went to close the door, she saw that the canary was fluttering around in an unusual manner and this caused her to go inside to investigate. On going into the lounge she saw Rose lying face down on a polished floor. Her head was close to the ottoman.

Upon hearing the evidence, the coroner decided to adjourn the hearing until the stomach contents of the dead woman could be analysed. He confirmed that there was no suggestion that anyone else was involved in the death of Rose, but wished to have full medical confirmation of that. At the resumed inquest in September, a verdict of accidental death was returned.

Bad weather in the Channel and the failure of the German air force to obtain superiority caused Hitler's plans for the invasion to be postponed. He instructed Goering to destroy the RAF and on 13 August 'Eagle Day' saw the beginning of a two-week assault on British air fields in an attempt to destroy the RAF on the ground.

On 12 August, however, the *Southampton Echo* printed a letter from the Mayor of Southampton, Mr Robert Sinclair, to the citizens of the town. In that letter, Mr Sinclair announced that it was his intention to initiate a fund that would collect money to pay for the building of a Spitfire which would be presented in the name of the people of the town.

Mr Sinclair went on to state that there was a special reason for doing this because the designer of the aeroplane, the late R.J. Mitchell, had, for a long time, been a resident of Southampton. The letter went on to say that the cost of such an aeroplane would be about £5,000 and although that was the initial target, it was hoped that the people of Southampton would enable the fund to exceed that of their neighbours in Portsmouth, who had raised over £11,000. Consequently, there would be a public meeting at the Polygon Hotel at which the fund would be officially launched.

Within a few days of the launch of the Spitfire Fund the total had already reached almost £500. Donations had been made by the Mayor and Mayoress but there had also been presentations from local businesses, sports organisations, school children and other citizens. The first street collection had taken place in Dimond Road, Bitterne Park when Mr Holmes had collected £2.14s. from his neighbours. Two schoolgirls had anonymously donated half a crown each and a football match took place at The Dell, and although there was no admission charge, a collection was organised at half-time. The largest individual donation to date had been £50 from Mr H.J. Holt.

It was on 24 August that a mistake helped to change Hitler's entire approach to the Battle of Britain. It was on that day that a German aircraft mistakenly dropped a bomb on a church in Cripplegate, London. Winston Churchill ordered that bombs be dropped on Berlin in retaliation. This, in turn led to the Germans stepping up their attacks on London. The Blitz was about to begin.

On 25 August, Mrs Isabel Barrett of Westwood Road reached the milestone of her 100th birthday. She had been born in Romsey but at the age of 10 had come to Southampton. Although her sight was somewhat impaired, she still had a sharp mind and took great interest

Isabel Barrett, who reached her 100th birthday on 25 August 1940.

in modern-day affairs. Despite a deterioration in her hearing, she still liked to listen to her favourite composers, Beethoven and Handel, on the radio but hated jazz, describing it as modern rubbish.

Interviewed by a reporter, she said that she had given up sugar and the journalist asked if this had taken place before the First World War. Mrs Barrett replied, 'Good gracious no! I gave it up after the Battle of Balaclava.' She also told the reporter that her mother lived to be 97 and an aunt lived until she was 96 but added, laughing, that she had beaten them both.

A strange story was told in the coroner's court on 2 September when inquiries were made into the death of 47-year-old Dorothy May Keene of Lumsden Avenue, Shirley. Mrs Keene, a spinster, lived with her brother, Leslie Owen Keene, who was nine years younger at 38.

It transpired that Dorothy had died from the effects of rat poison and when she was discovered, the police also found her brother in a starving and emaciated state. When asked why he had not reported his sister's death, Leslie had replied, 'I have no one to inform. I am waiting to die. I am unlucky. That's all.' He was then admitted to a mental hospital.

Percy William Keene, a brother of the couple, who lived in Pine Grove Road, Sholing, said he had not seen either Leslie or Dorothy in nine years and did not know where they were living until he read of the incident in the *Southampton Echo*.

Dr G.G. Havers had made a post-mortem examination of the dead woman and stated that at the time, Dorothy had been dead for at least a week. She had died from taking a corrosive phosphorus-based rat poison.

William Armstrong, a relief officer, stated that he had visited the couple on 6 July. He had told Dorothy that he had received reports that the couple were in need of either assistance or medical attention. Dorothy was neatly dressed at the time and stated that neither she nor her brother needed any help.

Southampton children evacuated to the countryside help with the harvest.

On 24 July, Herbert Frank Pipe, a county court bailiff had called at the address and spoken to Leslie. Asking after his sister, Leslie reported that she was sleeping but when Herbert saw her lying on the bed, he was sure that she was dead and contacted the police.

Constable Eric Coleman went to the address later the same day after speaking to Mr Pipe and found Leslie sitting in a chair and looking very ill. Going into the bedroom, Constable Coleman found Dorothy's body. She was fully clothed apart from her shoes. There was no food in the flat and only 5s. in cash.

After hearing all the evidence, an open verdict was returned. Leslie received the care he needed to get well both physically and mentally.

On 4 September, Southampton honoured and mourned a local hero, Acting Leading Seaman Jack Foreman Mantle of HMS *Foylebank* who had been awarded the Victoria Cross. Jack Mantle was only 23 and had lived at 2 Malvern Road, Shirley.

The official report into Jack's death stated that he had been in charge of the starboard pom-pom gun when his ship had been attacked by enemy aircraft on 4 July. Early in the action his left leg had been shattered by a bomb but he remained at his gun and continued firing. He was soon wounded again and eventually he fell by the gun and after the action was over, he was found to have died at his post.

Jack Mantle was one of six children and had joined the navy in 1934. At the time war broke out he was at the gunnery school in Portsmouth and had last been home on leave in May 1940, after which he was posted to HMS *Foylebank*.

Jack Mantle from Southampton, the recipient of the Victoria Cross.

Mr and Mrs Mantle had actually heard about the award of a Victoria Cross to their son from a neighbour. The announcement had been made over the radio and the neighbours had called around to tell them. It was later confirmed in an official communication. All the family were extremely proud of Jack.

By 10 September, Hitler had been forced to change his plans once more and Operation Sealion, the invasion of Britain, was postponed again. This time the proposed date was the 24th. Later it would be put back again, to the 27th, last day of the month with suitable tides.

On 14 September it was announced that the New Hippodrome was to close after that night's performance. The manager, Mr Richard Custance, stated that this closure was due to war conditions. The closing of this theatre meant that there was now only one live theatre left open in the town, the Palace. Before the war, there had been four such establishments; the Empire, the Palace, the Grand and, of course, the Hippodrome. The closing of the New Hippodrome meant that forty people lost their jobs.

At the end of September, Denis Albert Blackmore of Thackeray Road, Portswood pleaded 'Guilty under great provocation' to a charge of assaulting Alfred Andrew Winter. The problem began when about thirty people entered a public shelter during an air raid on the town. Some of the men wished to smoke and only one person, Mr Blackmore, objected. He stated loudly that the men should not smoke and asked the air-raid warden, Mr Pudney, to stop them from doing so. The warden replied that he did not have the power to do this, unless the atmosphere in the shelter became thick. This did not please Mr Blackmore who then complained that he wished to get some sleep as he had to get up early the next morning to do work of national importance.

By this time, many of the people down in the shelter were growing tired of the arguments and told Mr Blackmore to shut up. At this point, Mr Winter joined in saying that Blackmore was not the only man doing work of national importance. Blackmore then asked him to step outside so they could fight and when Winter refused, Blackmore struck him on the right side of the face. The blow was so fierce that Winter was knocked off his seat and fell to the floor, unconscious.

Blackmore now admitted to the court that he had gone too far and wished to apologise. Taking that into account, the magistrates ordered that Blackmore would have to pay court costs of £3.9s. which included 2 guineas solicitor's costs.

It was also at the end of September, on the 27th, that the Tripartite Pact was signed between Germany, Italy and Japan. This would provide mutual aid in the event of Japan entering the war. The pact was given an informal name, the Axis.

On 9 October, the Prime Minister, Neville Chamberlain, resigned from the House of Commons for health reasons. Winston Churchill was elected leader of the Conservative Party. Mr Chamberlain's health problems did not abate and he passed away on 9 November.

It was also in November that the Axis expanded. Initially, Russia was invited to sign the Tripartite Pact and did consider the offer, demanding substantial new territorial gains. However, on the 20th, Hungary did join. Three days later Romania also signed, to be followed on the 24th by the Slovak Republic.

In late November and early December, the town of Southampton was heavily bombed by the Luftwaffe and these events are detailed in the next chapter.

CHAPTER THREE

The Southampton Blitz

As an important port on the south coast of England, Southampton was a major target for the German Luftwaffe. In all, there were 57 separate bombing raids on the town which involved 1,605 air-raid alarms, 2,361 bombs dropped totalling some 475 tons of high explosives and about 31,000 incendiaries. These raids resulted in the deaths of 631 people with a further 898 seriously injured and 979 suffering relatively minor injuries. The damage inflicted was also considerable with 963 homes destroyed and a further 8,927 seriously damaged. Obviously, London and other locations such as Coventry were more heavily bombed but Southampton held the place as the seventh most bombed town in the country. It seemed that the authorities in the town expected war to come long before it actually did. It was in Southampton that the very first air-raid blackout exercise was conducted, as early as 1937.

The very first aerial attack upon the town occurred on 19 June 1940 during which a church was destroyed. After this there were a number of small attacks, sometimes specifically targeting the docks, the Supermarine Spitfire factory and railway lines, but the most severe attacks came to be known as the Southampton Blitz. This blitz took place over three nights, those of 23 November, 30 November and 1 December. These three raids destroyed a great deal of the town centre including seven churches. After this, there were only relatively minor raids, though one in June 1942 involved around fifty bombers. The attacks finally ended when two V1 rockets landed on the town.

The first daylight raid on the town took place on 13 August 1940 when the docks and the Spitfire factory were the main targets, however, the Cold Store, which was full of butter at the time, was also hit. The resulting fire burned for two weeks.

Initial reports stated that four people were killed but this was expected to rise as other victims might be buried underneath the rubble. The raid took place late in the afternoon. One of victims was

ARP workers clearing rubble after the bombing of the town.

14-year-old Harry Snell, who was found in the remains of his destroyed home with his puppy, Bob, still clasped in his arms. The dog was unhurt but Harry died from his injuries.

The landlord of a nearby public house had a remarkable escape. He and his wife were behind the counter when a bomb landed outside and blew out an entire wall. Debris was thrown into the pub but the couple were both completely unhurt.

Another of the casualties was 69-year-old Frederick William Foot who was working at the Pirelli General Cable Works. Mr Foot was not, however, killed by direct enemy action. He had suffered from heart problems for many years and during the raid he had a heart attack and died before he could receive medical attention.

The second daylight raid took place almost immediately afterwards, on 15 August. This time there were no fatalities but a railway worker had a fortuitous escape when a bomb hit the railway track just as his slow-moving train was travelling past. The bomb caused a crater in front of the train which then ploughed into it. Fortunately, the driver and passengers on the train were not hurt.

One of the most tragic events of the bombing of Southampton took place on 6 November. On that date only twelve bombs were dropped on the town but, at 2.45pm, one of them, a 500lb high-explosive device struck the art school. Some of the children had remained in their classroom whilst others took shelter in the basement. In fact, this had no protective value whatsoever as the bomb hurled through the roof and finally exploded in the basement itself. A total of fourteen children died and only one survived. His name was Andrew Bissell and he would later detail his experiences in his book *Southampton's Children of the Blitz*. Other people were killed by this same bomb and the final death toll was more than thirty.

The first police officer to be killed by enemy action was Constable Frederick Ernest Tupper. He was especially close to the Chief Constable, Mr Allen, as Constable Tupper had acted as his chauffeur since his appointment. He had also fulfilled this role for the previous Chief Constable, Mr McCormack, during the entire thirteen years he served. Constable Tupper left a wife and four children.

On 23 November, Joseph William Fletcher, a baker, was killed. He was loading his van in a side street when a bomb struck a nearby

The result of one bomb.

High Street after one of the raids.

building causing a wall to collapse. That wall fell onto Mr Fletcher who was later found buried underneath the rubble inside his wrecked van. Another casualty on that same date was Edgar Perry, who had once worked as a trimmer on board RMS *Titanic* in 1912. Edgar had survived the sinking, but died with his wife as they sheltered from the bombing.

The very worst of the bombing took place over the two nights of 30 November and 1 December. Amongst the dead were two recently married ARP men who died when a bomb fell near their fire engine. They had only been on duty a matter of seconds.

A convent, a nurse's home, the *Echo* newspaper office and a maternity home were amongst premises badly damaged. The enemy began by dropping incendiaries and then followed this with high explosives.

A hospital porter, Mr Wilkinson, saw an incendiary fall onto the roof of the hospital. Without a thought for his own safety, he then leapt from one roof, across a gap of more than 7ft, to deal with the device. He had nothing with him to use as a tool so picked up the bomb with his bare hands and dropped it over the roof. Later, on his way to have his hands dressed a bomb landed close to Mr Wilkinson and blew him into a flowerbed.

Other people were also fortunate. A group of around sixty evacuated a public house in order to go to a nearby shelter. They had just reached the shelter entrance when a bomb destroyed the pub they had been in. Another narrow escape took place when the police station received a direct hit. All the officers, except one, were out on duty otherwise the death toll would have been horrendous but one man, a sergeant, standing in a passageway was killed instantly.

Perhaps the luckiest escape belonged to the Chilver family and, once again, a dog played a vital part in saving at least one life. The entire family, Mr and Mrs Chilver and their two daughters aged 17 and 7, were in the shelter in their back garden when a high-explosive bomb landed a mere 15ft away. Part of the shelter collapsed and

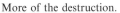

More of the destruction.

Members of the Auxiliary Fire Service practising during the period of the Southampton Blitz.

stones, bricks and other debris was thrown on top, burying all four occupants.

Mr Chilver managed to extricate himself with some degree of difficulty and was also able to free his eldest daughter. He then sent her for help and in the meantime began scrabbling at the debris with his bare hands. He knew that both his wife and youngest daughter were buried quite deeply and would be starved of oxygen. If he didn't get them out within a few minutes they would more than likely die from suffocation.

As he fought his way down the pile of rubble Mr Chilver called out for help. An ARP senior warden named William Cowie was positioned at a nearby post, and he heard the cry for help. So did Constable Trim who was on his beat. The two men came to Mr Chilver's aid and together they managed to free Mrs Chilver's face so that she was then able to breath. It was then that fortune took a hand.

When the family had first gone into the shelter the youngest girl had taken her pet, a Welsh corgi, with her. The dog was uninjured and had managed to tunnel its way through 4ft of dirt and rubble to the surface. This left a hole for oxygen to get down into the remains

Above Bar after the November raid.

The King visiting the town on 30 November.

of the shelter so that by the time the rescue team reached the youngest daughter, she was found alive and well.

All the injuries sustained by the family were minor ones but they were escorted to the ARP shelter to sit out the rest of the raid. As for Warden Cowie and Constable Trim, they went back on duty and some minutes later helped to free another family from their own shelter after it too was partly buried by debris.

The bombing raids on the town of Southampton left it changed forever. The city centre was very badly damaged with many beloved landmarks being lost for all time.

CHAPTER FOUR

1941

The year 1941 opened with a very sad, local story. Rosalind Mary Smith, aged just 22, of Portswood Road and a hairdresser by trade, had been found dead, on the railway line near Andover, having been decapitated. Her body had been found by a 13-year-old schoolboy. Close by the body was a handbag and Constable Preston said that upon looking inside, he had found two notes and a letter.

At the inquest, the dead girl's mother, Gladys Smith, told the court that her daughter had been treated for depression, nervous trouble and a lack of sleep, having been badly affected by the recent air raids. Recently, she had been caught in a raid and took cover in some premises which had been hit on the side by a bomb and this greatly troubled Rosalind. The doctor had advised that a change of scenery might do Rosalind good and, acting on that advice, she had caught a bus for Andover, to stay with her grandparents, but she had never reached their home and must have gone straight onto the railway where she had lain her head upon the line.

Rosalind had been engaged and was due to marry Mr Charles Hudson in March. The coroner returned a verdict that Rosalind had taken her own life whilst the balance of her mind was disturbed. A telegram had been sent to Mr Hudson, a serving soldier, to inform him of the death of his fiancée.

In mid-January German forces began bombing Malta. It was the beginning of a long campaign that would see the citizens of that island suffering badly but standing firm in the face of the enemy. It was also about the same time that it was announced that a brave 16-year-old Southampton girl had become the youngest recipient of the Order of the British Empire.

Evelyn Harmer of 48 Burgess Road, Bassett, was employed by the Phoenix Wharf and Coal Company of Belvidere Road, Northam in September 1940 when a daylight raid took place over the town.

Evelyn Harmer, awarded the OBE for her bravery during the Southampton Blitz.

A number of high-explosive bombs were dropped about 100yds from the company premises and Evelyn, along with the other members of staff, took cover in a nearby shelter.

The bombs continued to fall and at one stage an official entered the shelter and asked if anyone would volunteer to operate the switchboard so that messages could be relayed to the police and ARP officials. Evelyn immediately volunteered but her manager objected, saying that she was too young for such a hazardous task. Evelyn, however, was not to be dissuaded and eventually her manager gave way and the plucky girl returned to her switchboard despite the fact that the windows of the room had been blown in and there was debris all over the room.

Evelyn maintained her position for a full 3 hours and during that time another massive bomb exploded no more than 40yds away. The building shook violently but Evelyn did not even flinch.

Another official described her efforts thus, 'Miss Harmer's conduct undoubtedly contributed very largely to the success achieved by the ARP services in dealing with the conditions prevailing at that time.

She set a very high example of cool and selfless courage in circumstances and conditions which might have shaken the strongest nerves.'

This was not the first time that Evelyn had displayed courage in a time of trouble. When she was just 13 a friend had come over to stay and during the night Evelyn smelled smoke. Going downstairs she found a room on fire and single-handedly dealt with the blaze.

The report ended with the news that although Evelyn was not going to be 17 until 15 February, her parents had given their permission for her to be married and she would soon be travelling up to Aberdeen to marry Pilot Officer Stanley Jefferson who was serving in a Coastal Command unit.

Towards the end of January, the *Southampton Echo* published a report on theatres and other places of entertainment within the town and made it clear that these may well have been deliberate targets for German bombing raids.

Only two functioning theatres had remained within the town after the blitz and of these, one, the Palace, had since been demolished and the other, the New Hippodrome, had been badly damaged.

Seven cinemas had been closed as a result of the raids. The Picture House had been gutted by fire, the Forum wrecked by bombs and the Classic damaged by a raging fire. Meanwhile, the Lyric, the Woolston Picture House, King's and the Standard, though undamaged, had also been closed down.

The very first casualty had been the Picture House which had been burnt out in one of the earliest raids on the town. Next door to this had been the most recent addition to Southampton's places of entertainment, the Classic, where only the vestibule had been burnt but this still necessitated the building closing down.

The Forum was the next establishment to be hit and was now under repair. The manager hoped that the Forum might open again at around Easter time. On the night the Forum was hit there were over 1,000 people inside. The manager, Mr Scott-Buccleuch, ordered them all to the shelters as the raid commenced. Just 30 minutes after the theatre had been cleared a massive bomb crashed through the roof and landed near the stage where it exploded. Had it not been for the manager's action, many hundreds of people might have perished.

On 31 January, the citizens of Southampton were pleased to welcome the Prime Minster, Winston Churchill, to the town when he made a surprise visit. Late in the morning people passing the Civic

Centre saw the Civil Defence Forces on parade in the forecourt and a crowd soon gathered, wondering what was going on. They hadn't been waiting very long when an official looking car stopped and the familiar figure of Mr Churchill stepped out. He was immediately greeted with loud cheers.

The Prime Minister was met on the steps of the centre by the Mayor, Councillor Lewis, who introduced the Sheriff, Councillor Ponsford, and the ARP Controller, Captain Phillips, who called for the crowd to give Mr Churchill three cheers. The crowd did so with gusto. The Prime Minister then turned to the crowd and shouted, 'Are we downhearted?' A resounding 'No' was the reply.

After meeting local dignitaries inside the Civic Centre, Mr Churchill was then taken on a tour of the town by car. He spent a good deal of time at the docks before being driven to the station where he boarded a train to take him back to London.

It was on 8 February that the US House of Representatives passed the Lend-Lease Bill. This would be signed by President Roosevelt in early March meaning that the UK, China and other Allied nations could purchase military equipment and defer payment until after the war was over.

The UK, meanwhile, had been enjoying a great deal of success against the Italian forces in North Africa. This, in turn, had caused Hitler to decide that German aid would be given and on 11 February the first elements of the newly formed Afrika Korps under the command of Rommel landed in Tripoli. The first meeting between British and German forces would take place in Libya on the 20th of the month.

During the third week of February a Southampton heroine received the George Medal for her bravery during the bombing of the town.

Mary Joyce Newman, an 18-year-old assistant nurse of Magnolia Road, Bitterne, was off duty at the time but as the bombs rained down she went to assist a number of people. She saw a bomb strike two houses and rushed forward to see what she could do to help. In one of the houses, the four occupants had all been killed outright. In the second house, a man had been blown through his front door and after she had attended to him, Mary saw his son, a young man of 19, hanging upside down, trapped by his ankles. Mary crawled through a narrow hole to comfort him and offer him assistance for over an hour, despite the fact that gas was escaping from a shattered main and at one stage she was almost overcome by the fumes.

When the incident was over, Mary ran on to her place of work, realising that she would be late but she had been given a note by an ARP official to explain why. Interviewed by the local newspaper, Mary explained, 'The gas made me feel sleepy. Once one of the rescue squad trod on my toe and woke me up. I didn't feel the effects much until the following afternoon.'

In March, the UK broke off diplomatic relations with Bulgaria and the following month, Moscow reported that German troops were in Finland. Later that report was amended to show that in fact they were using the country to approach Norway. An invasion was imminent.

Erwin Rommel's first real offensive against the British took place on 24 March at El Agheila in Libya. It was a great success for the German forces who caused the British to retreat. Within three weeks British troops would be driven back to Egypt. This culminated in Rommel capturing Benghazi on 3 April. Only Tobruk was retained by the British, and this would remain a thorn in the side of the Afrika Korps for many months to come.

A direct attack on Tobruk took place on 14 April but Rommel was forced to retreat. Another British success took place the very next day when the navy intercepted an Afrika Korps convoy. All five troop transports and three Italian destroyers who were escorting were sunk.

An event that received no publicity at the time but would help with one of the greatest coups of the war took place on 9 May. It was on that day that the German submarine *U110* was captured by the Royal Navy in the Atlantic. The vessel's cryptography code machine, the 'Enigma', was captured intact, along with the code book. Behind the scenes this would eventually help British code-breakers at Bletchley Park to break all the German codes.

A most curious incident was reported in May and it is one that remains the subject of debate even today. On 10 May, Rudolph Hess, Hitler's deputy, flew to Scotland. He was soon captured by a plough-man, David McClean, and handed over to the authorities. It has been suggested that Hess had come to negotiate a peace between the UK and Germany. In return for being allowed to keep her Empire, the UK was to agree to give Germany a free reign in the East. If true, this would clearly be an attempt to eliminate the UK as a threat before the invasion of Russia.

On 24 May, HMS *Hood* had been sunk by the *Bismarck* in the Atlantic. This had been a terrible blow to British morale. Out of a complement of 1,418 men, there were only 3 survivors, Ordinary Signalman Ted Briggs, Able Seaman Robert Tilburn and Midshipman William John Dundas. By 5 June, a total of thirty men from Southampton were listed as fatalities from the *Hood* and one of these was Petty Officer Frederick George Sheppard of Mayfield Road, who, a few months previously, had been one of the men who had shown the Prime Minister, Mr Churchill, around when he visited the ship. The *Bismarck* would be attacked and sunk just two days after the *Hood* had been lost.

It was also in June that George Formby made an appearance at the Regal in Southampton. At about the same time there were rumours that Hitler was planning an invasion of Russia but these were largely discounted. Surely such a thing was unthinkable as the two countries had signed a non-aggression pact. Perhaps of more local import at the time was that clothes rationing had been introduced on 1 June.

There was a link with the First World War of on 4 June when it was announced that the former emperor Kaiser Willem II had died in the Netherlands. Eleven days later, on the 15th, the British attempted to relieve the siege of Tobruk. The operation failed and the British suffered a heavy defeat at Halfaya Pass which the troops renamed Hell-Fire Pass.

The unthinkable happened on 22 June when Operation Barbarossa, the invasion of the Soviet Union by German forces, began. The initial operation was a three-pronged attack aiming at Moscow, Leningrad and the southern oilfields. Events then moved rapidly with Romanian troops invading southern Russia. They were joined on 26 June by Hungary and Slovakia declaring war on Russia and, after Russian planes had bombed Helsinki, Finland also declared war.

There was a double dose of bad news for the town's citizens in early July. On the 2nd it was announced that there were beer shortages and that many public houses were on restricted opening hours. Less than a week later, on 7 July, the price of the *Southampton Echo* was raised from 1*d.* to 1½*d.*

On 22 July a trial for manslaughter opened at Winchester, before Mr Justice Charles. A sailor, Robert McClyments McGhee, aged 22, was charged with shooting a fellow seaman, Kenneth Aubrey Smith, at Southampton docks. On the day in question, 17 June, McGhee had been working as a messenger to the Quartermaster, Leading Seaman

Whyke. That evening Smith, Whyke and McGhee were all in conversation together. The three were enjoying a joke when the Quartermaster remarked that Smith was looking rather pale. Smith had replied, 'Yes, I know.' To this, McGhee replied, 'I will soon cure you.' Smith then answered with 'Shoot me' at which point a shot rang out.

Evidence was given by Lieutenant Daniel Ungoed that McGhee was not asustomed to handling firearms and, indeed, had never used one before that day. Whyke confirmed that at the time of the shooting, McGhee and Smith were laughing, joking and on the best of terms.

After hearing all the testimony, including McGhee's account that he had no intention of shooting Smith, Mr Justice Charles told the jury that he had seen no evidence that there had been any negligence that would amount to a crime and that therefore the prosecution had not made out an adequate case for a verdict of manslaughter to be returned. The jury, having listened to that summing up, duly returned a verdict of not guilty and McGhee left court a free man.

There was another important court case at the end of July when Edward Cecil Smith appeared before the magistrates in Southampton, charged with wilfully making a false declaration for the purpose of procuring a marriage. Smith, who was 39, was attempting to marry a 16-year-old girl and he had described himself as a bachelor on his notice of marriage form when in fact he was already married.

Gladys Berry, the deputy registrar of births, deaths and marriages, told the court that Smith called at the office on 25 April and gave notice of his intention to marry Joyce Petcher on 25 May. He described himself as a bachelor and signed the form to that effect.

Leonard Stanley Smith, who was a brother of the defendant, stated that he was a witness to the marriage of Edward to Mary Elizabeth Veronica Cousins on 1 January 1927.

The next witness was Detective Constable Stanley Dunn who stated that on 27 June, Edward Smith had handed him a written statement which began,

I had just returned to England after spending five years in India without coming into contact with any white women, when I met Mrs Cousins, who made advances to me. She told me that she was a widow, but had a son by her late husband, who was a sergeant in the RAMC and that he, the husband, was killed in France.

She asked me to marry her, and, seeing that she would be giving up her widow's pension, I really thought it my place to marry her, considering I have a great respect for the opposite sex.

I was hurried into the marriage by her wish, and it was years afterwards that I found out that she had told me a lie, because the money she was receiving was from a former man friend and he was the father of her son.

Seeing I could find no information about her previous husband I assumed that she had never been married before. Therefore, I considered I was not legally married.

Having heard this evidence, the bench pointed out that even though his wife might have described herself as a widow when in fact she was single, this did not invalidate that marriage. Consequently, Smith was found guilty as charged and was fined £10 and ordered to pay £2.7s. costs.

However, there was a twist to the story in that between making the false declaration and appearing in court, Smith's wife had passed away meaning that had he waited just a little longer, no offence would have been committed.

Though no one could know it at the time, in Europe an important decision had been made by Adolf Hitler. On the last day of July, he had ordered Hermann Goering to appoint SS General Reinhard Heydrich to submit plans for the final solution to the Jewish question.

On 1 August, a man posing as a bogus collector of charitable contributions was captured when he called at the house of a police constable and attempted to get the officer to contribute. William John Roberts, 29, of Warwick Street, Southsea, pleaded guilty to attempting to obtain a contribution on behalf of the Red Cross from Beatrice Maud Mary Cooper of 290 Portswood Road on 23 July. He was also charged with obtaining 1s. from Thomas Henry Brooking, at the Waggoner's Arms, Portswood Road, and 6d. each from William Arthur Keleher and Reginald Kelsey

It so happened that Mrs Cooper's husband was a police constable. He asked Roberts to produce his authority to collect on behalf of the fund and Roberts was arrested when he couldn't do so. Roberts claimed that he had no intention to defraud. He lived in Basingstoke and was on holiday in Southampton when he heard of a cricket match to be played to raise funds for the Red Cross. He decided to collect for the fund when he ran into trouble.

A Home Guard recruitment march through the town in the autumn of 1941.

Chief Inspector Ward told the court that Roberts had numerous convictions for petty larceny, since 1928. These included a sentence of three years, at Portsmouth, in January 1933. His last conviction was also at Portsmouth in February 1941. Found guilty, Roberts was sentenced to six months' hard labour and was declared a rogue and a vagabond.

It was also in August that there were rumblings of discontent from the Japanese government. They had been in discussions with the US over various trade and military agreements. These had apparently now reached a stalemate and, rather ominously, the Japanese authorities had commented, 'It is now time for Japan to complete her preparations in anticipation of the worst to come.'

On 5 August, a sad story finally came to an end with the discovery of the body of Miss Margaret Sargeaunt, who had been missing since 27 July. Her body was discovered in the River Test at Greatbridge, by some soldiers on exercise. Margaret had left home to go for a walk on the 27th and when she did not return the police were informed and a massive search, which included police dogs, was instigated.

Margaret Sargeaunt, who sadly took her own life in August 1941.

It was stated that Margaret was home on leave from her work in Liverpool, where she held a responsible position. She had worked long hours and had been through some of the worst air raids that Liverpool had suffered. She had also been doing extra work for the ARP. Margaret was a highly intelligent woman and spoke Dutch, French and German in addition to her native English. Her workload and the stress of the bombing had preyed upon her mind and it was believed that she had finally succumbed to that pressure and taken her own life.

During the month of September an event occurred that received little publicity at the time but would reinforce American attitudes toward the Axis powers and to the war itself. On the 4th the American ship USS *Greer* was fired upon by a German U-boat. There were no casualties but the event did serve to increase tensions between the US and Germany.

In late September, an inquest opened into the tragic death of a 5-year-old boy named Brian Henry Hoare, who had been killed on his way home from school the previous week. Brian had been playing tag with a friend when he stepped off the pavement in Margam Avenue, Sholing, into the path of a bus driven by Leonard Frank Collins. Brian was very badly injured and died later that same day in the Royal South Hants and Southampton Hospital.

Rose Booth had been a witness to the terrible event. She testified that the boy Brian was playing with was bigger than him and at one stage Brian simply stepped out in front of the bus which was travelling at a very moderate speed. Leonard Collins, the driver, told the court that the bus was actually a school bus, carrying seventy-three children from the Magnolia Road School. He estimated that he was doing between 10 and 15mph at the time of the accident. He had seen Brian step out a few yards in front of the bus and immediately applied his brakes but the offside wing had struck the child.

A verdict of accidental death was returned and the coroner, Mr Arthur Emanuel, stated that no blame whatsoever should be attached to the driver.

In the same month of September, the Americans made their own comments on the breakdown of the talks with Japan. Many Americans believed that war was imminent. And the isolationists were, as a result, becoming very alarmed. The author Edgar Rice Burroughs summed up the mood of many people when he wrote, 'The general feeling here is that America will be in the war quite soon and while no one anticipates it with any degree of pleasure, the majority are courageously resigned to it.'

A local tragedy was detailed in early October. Retired clergyman, the Revd Algernon Cooper, 54, had gassed himself at the home of his friends in Winchester Road, Southampton. He had left a letter behind which read, in part, 'This awful war in which there seems so little that one can do. I have lost all my friends, so what is there to live for? The world's grief, reflected in the faces of the crowd, is too much for me.'

Another event that affected American attitudes took place on 17 October when the destroyer USS *Kearny* was torpedoed by the *U568* off the coast of Iceland. This time there were casualties and eleven sailors lost their lives. They were the first American servicemen killed by Germany but worse was to come. On the 31st, another destroyer, USS *Reuben James*, was also torpedoed near Iceland. More than 100 sailors were killed and the warship was lost.

What might turn out to be the final chance of avoiding war between the US and Japan were talks in November between Mr Saburo Kurusu and Mr Cordell Hull, the US Secretary of State. Both sides referred to them as 'peace or war' talks. In fact, Japan had already decided on her course of action and this was seen by Joseph Grew, the US ambassador to Japan, who sent a cable to the State Department clearly asserting that Japan had plans to launch an attack against Pearl Harbor. The authorities chose to ignore the message.

On 5 December, a terrible story was revealed in the Southampton coroner's court. On the 2nd of the month, 7-year-old Mary Angell and her 5-year-old sister Nellie, who lived at 14 Bedbridge Hill, Old Shirley, had been given a sixpence each by their mother so that they could buy some paper chains to decorate their home for Christmas.

The two girls were delighted with their colourful purchases and were excitedly looking at them, near the fireplace. Little Nellie was standing close to the fire with a paper chain hanging over her shoulder and down her back. The chain caught fire and this in turn set fire to Nellie's coat. Bravely, Mary pulled her sister's blazing coat off her but by this time the child's hair and dress were also on fire.

Nellie ran out of the house, screaming and a gentleman passing by came to her assistance, tearing off her clothes and trying to smother the flames. A neighbour, hearing the commotion, brought out a blanket and wrapped the badly injured child in it before taking her to the Children's Hospital in Shirley but sadly Nellie died the following day.

A momentous event occurred on 7 December when the predicted attack on Pearl Harbor took place. The next day, 8 December, the Japanese invaded Thailand. There were also attacks on Hong Kong, Guam and the Philippines and Singapore was bombed. Two days later, on the 10th, HMS *Prince of Wales* and HMS *Repulse* were sunk in an attack near Malaya. Eight days later, on 18 December, a new National Service Act extended conscription to all men and women. Everyone was now expected to do some form of national service which included military service for men under 51 and also for unmarried women between 20 and 30 years of age.

Just before Christmas, on 22 December, the *Southampton Echo* reported the story of a family who had suffered much. Within the space of just over two months, Mr and Mrs Moss of 15 Kingsley Road, Millbrook, learned of the death of three of their sons. In October, the deaths at sea of Reginald James Moss and Stanley Victor Moss were announced. They were both firemen in the same ship, the SS *Seagem*.

Now they had just been notified of the death of Torpedo Petty Officer George Frederick Moss, 37, who was killed at sea, on 25 November, whilst serving with the Royal Navy on HMS *Barham*. He was married and had a son whom he had never seen. Two more sons were still serving; one in the army and one in the Merchant Navy.

George, the third son lost by Mr and Mrs Moss at the end of 1941.

On Christmas Day, Hong Kong finally fell to the Japanese. It was just the latest in a number of setbacks. The year 1941 had been a terrible one for the UK and the Allies and it seemed that there was little, if any, good news on the horizon.

CHAPTER FIVE

1942

The bad news continued throughout January 1942. On the 2nd, Japanese forces captured Manila. They advanced throughout Borneo, meeting little opposition, during the early weeks of the year and captured Kuala Lumpur on the 11th, with many British soldiers taken north of Singapore. Meanwhile, in North Africa, Rommel was continuing to advance and Benghazi was recaptured by the Germans.

Two young men appeared before the magistrates on 15 January charged with being absent without leave from their ship. They both pleaded guilty to the offence. Alex Hill, 19, and his friend, 18-year-old Edward Robertson, both from Southampton, were serving on a ship in an unnamed Welsh port when they were both given one day's leave. They were allowed to leave at 6.30am on 5 January and were due to report back at the same time the following day. Both men returned 24 hours late, at 6.30am on the 7th.

The men explained that they had been to visit friends of Hill's in Barry. He was employed as a mess boy and as a result of his absence the Chief Steward had to do his work. Robertson was employed as a cabin boy. Hill and Robertson were both fined £3 and put on probation until those fines were paid in full. In addition, Hill, who had been described as lazy and inefficient, was also dismissed from his post.

At a meeting on 21 January a proposal from the Transport Committee was accepted by the Borough Council. The suggestion had been to allow passengers on public transport to act as auxiliary conductors. It was explained that there would need to be a full consultation with existing staff before the scheme could be implemented but Alderman Bowyer, the chairman of the Committee, stated that the original idea had actually been put forward by the trades unions themselves and all the staff were very pleased with the idea.

News of a local tragedy was reported towards the end of January 1942. At about 5.30am on the 19th, Mrs Day of 70 Bellemoor Road

The British Empire rallied to the country's aid. This is a relief car donated by the people of Barbados.

woke to find that her husband was not in bed next to her. Going downstairs to investigate, she found a handwritten note pinned to the scullery door. It read 'Beware, gas'. Mrs Day opened the door and found her husband, 55-year-old Ernest, lying on the floor, the room filled with gas and a tube fixed to the stop-cock of a stove. She immediately turned off the gas and summoned a doctor but it was too late, her husband was already dead. The report stated that Mr Day had been an invalid for the past six years and that his depression over this might have led him to take his own life.

In February, the death of 70-year-old nightwatchman and old-age pensioner William Nolan Burnand was inquired into by the coroner. Mr Burnand, who had good eyesight but rather poor hearing, was on his way to his duty at the Cowherds Inn and as he walked there, down The Avenue, he was struck by a motorcycle ridden by Edward George Foreman, of Evans Street.

The accident was witnessed by Reginald George Link who told the inquest that Mr Foreman was cycling on the correct side of the road and at no more than 15 to 20mph. Mr Burnand seemed to stumble a little just before the cycle struck him and afterwards he began to try to crawl along the footpath. Mr Link ran to his aid and heard the injured man say, 'I did not see the car [sic] until it hit me.'

The injured man was taken to hospital where he was treated by Dr D. Malcombe but despite receiving treatment, Mr Burnand died a few days later from a pulmonary embolism following a fracture of his left leg. A verdict of accidental death was returned and the coroner stated that no blame should be attached to the motorcyclist.

In the middle of February, Singapore finally fell to the Imperial Japanese forces and on the 19th, Darwin, in Australia's Northern Territory, was bombed by the Japanese air force. Back at home it was the turn of soap to be rationed and on the 25th of the month it was announced that Princess Elizabeth, the heir to the throne, had registered for war service.

At the end of February, George William Cull of Hammonds Lane, Totton and his friend Alfred Edward Bumford appeared in court to face charges of stealing 200,000 cigarettes with a total value of £716, the property of the Southern Railway Company.

The cigarettes were taken from the Millbrook goods station on 9 February and there were two further charges to answer. The first was the stealing of an additional 260,000 cigarettes valued at £923 on 5 February. The second charge was one of stealing a motor car, valued at £120, from William MacArtney Read, from the car park of the Polygon Hotel, on 12 January. Both men received sentences of imprisonment.

On 11 March, the death of Squadron Leader Eric Verdon-Roe was announced. He was the eldest son of Sir Alliott Verdon-Roe and his wife of The Cockpit, Fair Oak, Eastleigh. The Squadron Leader had originally been listed as missing in action the previous July, but was now presumed to be dead. Verdon-Roe had only been 16 years old when he first took a flying course at the Hampshire Aerodrome Club, and quickly obtained his pilot's licence. In due course he joined the RAF, and was commissioned as Acting Pilot Officer on 16 March 1934. He was subsequently promoted to Flying Officer in 1936, Flight Lieutenant in 1938 and Squadron Leader in 1940. At the time of his death he was still only 25 and was the youngest officer of his rank in the RAF.

Verdon-Roe had been piloting a bomber on the day he went missing. He radioed in to say that his aircraft was badly damaged and he was then 80 miles from land, over the North Sea. It was his thirtieth bombing flight. The dead man had two younger brothers, both of whom were also serving in the RAF.

A most unusual case was considered by the coroner on 19 March. It related to the death of an electrician, 61-year-old John Osmund Newell of 351 Winchester Road, Bassett.

On the day in question, Mr Newell was working on a ship in Southampton docks. His job was to fit a total of thirty fans in various areas of the ship and he had already completed half. Number 16 was no different to the rest. Mr Newell had climbed up some steps and fitted the fan to the spindle by means of a nut which he then tightened. The fan consisted of two large aluminium blades, each some 18in in length and, just as he had done with the previous fifteen, Mr Newell then took hold of one of the blades and spun it rapidly in order to see that it was free to move on the spindle. Unfortunately, this time he must have been a little bit higher up the steps for the second blade whirled around and struck him in the back of the head.

The injured man climbed down from the steps and told his assistant, William John Cooper Hayden, that he felt dizzy. He was given first aid at the scene and then taken to hospital. Dr Theodore Bliss could find no sign whatsoever of any external injury on the back of Mr Newell's head but he steadily got worse and finally passed away the same day. A subsequent post-mortem revealed that despite there being no signs of any violence externally, the man's brain had been injured and he had died from a laceration of the base of the brain and subsequent bleeding internally. A verdict of accidental death was returned.

Mrs Fellowes of 8 Roberts Road in Southampton was excitedly waiting for a telegram from her husband. He was Stoker Stephen John Fellowes, serving in the Merchant Navy and due home on leave. On such occasions he would always send a telegram home to tell his wife when she could expect him to arrive.

The telegram arrived on 23 March and Mrs Fellowes opened it excitedly but to her horror the message was from the Admiralty, stating that her husband was missing, presumed killed. This was followed shortly afterwards by a second message confirming that his body had been recovered from the waters off Aberdeen. Stephen was only 28 when he died and was given a funeral with full military honours. His widow and their 18-month-old daughter attended.

At the end of March, the coroner, Arthur Emanuel, chaired a case that he described as a conundrum. He was inquiring into the death of 22-year-old Frederick George Cheer, a private in the Home Guard, who had been discovered in a bedroom at his home, 14 Glen Road, Woolston, dying from a rifle-shot wound.

Frank Cheer, the dead man's father, testified that his son, who had been a shipyard driller, had had a service rifle and ten rounds of ammunition for about a month. After his death, only nine rounds were found in a drawer. Frank had last seen his son alive at about 9.15pm on Sunday night when he was playing darts in the Grove public house on Swift Road. He was sober at the time. Frank had gone to bed at about 10.30pm that night. Not long afterwards he was woken by a loud report, followed by a thud. He went into his son's bedroom and found Frederick lying on the floor with a severe wound to his head.

The next witness was Dr J.A. Guilfoyle who had been on duty at the Royal South Hants and Southampton Hospital at the time. He stated that Frederick had died within 25 minutes of being admitted. The top part of his head had been shot away.

Ena Bailey, 22, of Church Road said that she had been seeing Frederick for about a year and they had become engaged last Christmas Eve. She had been with her fiancé in the Grove before returning to her house. Asked if they had had any arguments lately, Ena said that they had only been about very minor things such as him wanting to go to the pictures when she didn't want to. She also admitted, however, that Frederick had asked her if she wished to break off the engagement and she had told him that she didn't wish to. She had no idea why Frederick should have wanted to take his own life.

Percy Arthur Cheer was the dead man's younger brother and shared a bedroom with him. He testified that when he went to bed on the fateful night, Frederick's rifle was standing near the fireplace. He was woken later by the sound of a shot and saw his brother lying on the bedroom floor.

Captain Cyril Joseph Martin was Frederick's commanding officer in the Home Guard and he told the court that Frederick had been a good shot and knew how to handle his rifle. He saw no way that Frederick could have accidentally shot himself and saw no reason why he should kill himself.

In his summing up, the coroner said that the circumstances pointed to suicide but there seems to be no valid reason for Frederick to have taken his own life. His problems and concerns, such as they were, all seemed to be very minor ones. He felt that the only possible verdict was an open one.

It was also in March that electricity, coal and gas were rationed in Britain. In addition, the clothing ration was reduced.

On 3 April, Gunner William Arthur West RA, aged 32, was sent to prison for three months by Southampton magistrates. West had pleaded guilty to damaging two windows at the Assistance Board offices in Hill Lane on 20 March. He was also charged with assaulting Samuel Frank Curtis and Alfred Henry Hosgood at the same place.

Mr H.P. Roe for the prosecution said West had applied for supplementary allowance for his wife and family and called at the offices on 20 March in a very bad temper. He was shouting about the means test. He continued to yell and suddenly picked up a chair and threw it through the window. Curtis and Hosgood entered the room and West said, 'You two are just my handwriting'. He first hit Curtis and then Hosgood, who went to help Curtis, was thrown to the floor. After a violent struggle West was finally subdued.

Roe told the court West had a grievance against the military authorities and admitted he went to the office to cause trouble. Chief inspector Ward told the court that West was a local man who was on seven days' leave at the time of the offence.

It was also in April, on the 15th, that the brave island of Malta was awarded the George Cross for its heroism and devotion.

On the evening of 9 May, Dr Ernest Henry Murly Stancomb MB ChM collapsed whilst playing cards with a friend at his home, and died 15 minutes later. Dr Stancomb was in his 83rd year and had been in bad health, but recently had appeared to rally. He originally hailed from Coker in Somerset, but had moved to Southampton in 1885. He had been the oldest practising doctor in Southampton for many years before his recent retirement. He was an influential public speaker and became prominent in the town with his campaign for feeding hungry schoolchildren. He had been associated with the Labour Party, but had stood as Independent Health candidate in the 1922 parliamentary election in Southampton.

In Asia, on 20 May, the Japanese completed their conquest of Burma. It was announced as a military catastrophe as it now gave direct access to India. That, surely, would be the next target for the invading Japanese.

At the end of May, the *Echo* detailed a story of a stolen uniform, three robberies and a cheeky thief who dressed himself in the items he had stolen.

The uniform belonged to an RAF flying officer who had it specially made for his forthcoming wedding. He had been to Messrs J. Baker and Co. of 23 Queens Terrace for the fitting and expected to pick the suit up when he returned on leave for his marriage. Fortunately, the tailor still had all the measurements and rapidly made a second uniform. The officer was then given special leave to fly back from his station to have a second fitting and all was ready for the big day.

The thief, whoever he was, had gained entry to the tailors by removing the glass in a skylight and dropping down into the shop. After stealing the original uniform, along with twenty clothing coupons, he calmly let himself out through the front door, leaving it wide open.

Curiously, at about the same time that Baker's shop in Queens Terrace was being broken into, someone else broke into their branch in Portsmouth Road, Woolston. He helped himself to a grey sports coat, a pair of grey flannel trousers, a raincoat, two roll-neck pullovers and a quantity of ties and bows. The cheeky thief then discarded his own shabby brown coat, a stained shirt and some dirty grey trousers and left the shop, presumably dressed in his new finery.

This thief, however, then had the temerity to break into a shoe merchant a few doors down and stole boots and shoes to the value of £40. Once again he took the time to change for he left a tatty old pair of shoes behind.

At the beginning of June, ATS Corporal Joan Tambling, whose parents lived at 33 Chatsworth Road in Bitterne, won a most unusual accolade. Joan had always been careful to look her best and had, before the war, had ambitions to be a hairdresser. Now she had won first place in a smartest hair in the ATS competition.

Joan had volunteered for the services in October 1941 and had only been promoted to corporal a month ago. She now served as a telephonist on a gun site and also acted as an instructor in physical education.

It was also in early June a verdict of accidental death was returned at an inquest upon an 81-year-old widow, Annie Wilson, of Portsmouth Road, Woolston. The dead woman's daughter, Annie Heighway, stated that on the afternoon of her death, Mrs Wilson, who was paralysed in both legs, said that she felt cold and asked for the electric fire to be lit.

The fire was switched on and left a few feet away from where Annie Wilson was sitting. The daughter then left the room for a few minutes but after about 5 minutes she smelled burning. Going back into her mother's room she found her on the floor in a huddled position, with her back to the fire. Her clothing was smouldering and Annie was unconscious. Mrs Wilson was rushed to hospital where she was treated by Dr Theodore Bliss who reported that she had died soon after admission. The cause of death was shock, resulting from extensive burns.

It was also in June that the first reports began to filter through that poison gas was being used to kill Jews that the Germans claimed had been sent to the East for resettlement. On the 9th of the month the Czech village of Lidice was liquidated as a reprisal for the killing of Reinhard Heydrich the previous month. Nine days after this, on the 18th, a certain project was set up in the US which would later have worldwide significance. This was the Manhattan Project, the quest for the creation of an atomic bomb.

The middle of July saw the trial of Able Seaman Edward Thomas Lee open at Winchester. Lee, of 34 Imperial Avenue, Millbrook, was charged with the murder of Vera Margaret Bicknell, of 45 Cannon Street, Shirley, on 15 April. Lee was a married man but had been seeing Miss Bicknell for some time. He had tried to obtain a divorce so that he could marry his new-found love but when his wife refused his request, Lee then killed his girlfriend on Southampton Common.

It was alleged that at 11.10pm on the night of Miss Bicknell's death, Lee had knocked on the door of the Bellemoor Inn in Hill Lane and asked the landlord, Edgar Cameron Gordon Davidson, if he might use the telephone. Given permission to do so he then rang for an ambulance and the police, explaining that he had found a woman on the common. A police car arrived and Lee climbed into vehicle so that he could point out to the officers where the woman lay. On the way, Lee was asked by Sergeant Browne how he came to find the woman and he replied, 'I killed her.' He was immediately cautioned. Later, after showing the police where Miss Bicknell's body was, he again stated that he was responsible for her death.

At his trial a number of letters that Lee had written to the dead girl were read out in court. In one, dated 4 March, he had written, 'I cannot imagine living without you now, dearest. In fact, I wouldn't, so you can see how I feel.' In another, on 10 March, he had said, 'Forgive me for asking you that rotten question, darling, but, you see, the thought of anyone else ever having anything to do with you drives me nearly frantic.'

When Lee was arrested other letters, still sealed, were found on his person. One was addressed to his wife and this read in part, 'No doubt you have enjoyed the situation up to now. I don't blame you for being bitter, but I do blame you for being unreasonable. Well, see if you can get any fun out of this situation.'

Medical evidence was given by Dr James M. Webster who had performed the post-mortem on Miss Bicknell and testified that death was due to strangulation. Dr A.J. Grimson had examined Lee at the police station. He noted scratches of recent origin on the prisoner's chest and on his right cheek. He appeared to be perfectly lucid and certainly realised the gravity of the situation he was in.

For the defence, Mr Denning said that he would ask the jury to return a verdict of either guilty but insane, or guilty to manslaughter, not murder. He explained that Lee had a good service record and had volunteered for service just two days after war had been declared. He had joined the navy and served on a destroyer, seeing action in the seas off Norway, Holland and in the Mediterranean. His ship had been sunk and whilst engaged in the evacuation of Crete he had sustained an injury to his head.

Lee then entered the box to give evidence on his own behalf. He began by saying that he had been employed by a firm of cake makers when war broke out and had joined up as soon as he could. After detailing his time in the navy, Lee confirmed that he had returned to England in July 1941. He had known Miss Bicknell for some time and had started to spend time with her. Soon he was posted to Scotland but whilst travelling north he alighted from the train at Guildford, caught a train back to Portsmouth and then a second one back to Southampton.

On the day of Miss Bicknell's death, 15 April, they met up and towards the end of the evening he explained to her that his wife was still refusing to divorce him. Miss Bicknell then said that life was difficult for her. Lee replied that it was difficult for him too as he would have to give up his wife and child. They argued and she slapped his face. The next thing he remembered was sitting on the grass next to her with his hands around her throat. He had no memory of killing her.

After evidence had been given to the effect that Lee was not suffering from any form of insanity, the court adjourned for the day. On the following day, in his summing up, Mr Justice Charles clearly indicated that there was not a shred of evidence to support a verdict of manslaughter. The jury retired to consider their verdict and were out for 90 minutes. The clerk of the court asked, 'Do you find the prisoner guilty or not guilty of murder?' The foreman replied, 'Guilty of manslaughter'.

The judge appeared to be dumbstruck. He commented, 'I don't quite know what to say. I directed the jury that it was not open to them to find manslaughter. They have, in defiance of that direction and in falsity of their oaths, found that verdict.' He then turned to the jury and commented, 'You can leave the box now; you are not fit to be there.' He then sentenced Lee to fourteen years in prison.

The case of an imitation public house came before the magistrates on 20 August. Reginald Frederick Hoskins, the proprietor of the Windsor Social Club on Commercial Road, was charged with selling intoxicating liquor without being in possession of a valid licence. Charged with aiding and abetting him was Vera Maynard of Derby Road. Both parties pleaded guilty to the charges against them, Hoskins admitting twelve separate charges which took place between 20 and 24 July.

The club had been a concern for some time and in July police officers attended the club and, despite the fact that they were not members, they were able to purchase drinks without any problems. As a result of their investigation, the club was raided on 24 July and a large quantity of liquor was seized. Despite this, Hoskins managed to get fresh supplies and carried on trading before his eventual arrest.

Vera Maynard was held to be little more than a tool, used by Hoskins, and was only fined £5. Hoskins tried to explain to the court that he had been unaware that a licence was needed to sell liquor but that defence was soon negated by the fact that he had also been fined £5 in 1940 for selling drinks without a licence. He was sentenced to six months' imprisonment.

In September two employees at a Southampton factory were each fined £15 plus £1.1s. court costs for absenteeism and lateness for work. The two men were Cecil Montague Webb of Forster Road and Thomas George Cash of Arnold Road. Webb was summoned for being absent from work on 18 and 25 July and being persistently late between 6 and 20 May. He pleaded not guilty but Cash admitted charges of being absent on 11 April, 23 May and 30 June.

In the case against Webb, Frederick George Davis, the works superintendent, explained that Webb was employed as a rubber mixer. The dates of his being absent were confirmed and details of his lateness during the other period were given. He had persistently been late by around 15 to 20 minutes each day. He was interviewed in August and could give no valid reason for his offences. In court Webb claimed that he had been made ill by the work but this was not accepted by the magistrates as Webb had made no attempt to get a medical certificate to that effect.

Turning to Cash, the magistrates had heard that when first spoken to he had promised to improve his work standards and had been given four weeks' grace in which to do so. This had not, however, happened and consequently he was now appearing in court.

A significant event took place on 5 September when Australian and US forces combined at Milne Bay, Papua, to attack the occupying Japanese. It resulted in the first defeat for Japanese land forces in the war. This defeat, and the inability of the Japanese to build an airbase there, greatly relieved the threat to mainland Australia and showed that the enemy was not invincible.

The story of Jack Mantle of 2 Malvern Road winning the Victoria Cross in July 1940 has already been told (see p. 57). Jack, it will be recalled, lost his life manning a gun on HMS *Foylebank* whilst the ship was under enemy attack. Now, two years later, in October 1942, his brother, Sergeant Peter Mantle, was awarded the Military Medal for his actions in an incident in the Middle East. Although Peter was a son of Southampton, he had since emigrated to New Zealand and won his medal serving with the forces of that country.

Sergeant Peter Mantle who won the Military Medal after his brother had won the Victoria Cross.

On 16 October an inquest into the death of 19-year-old Douglas Edward Jones was heard at Southampton. Douglas had lived at 56 Lilac Road in Bassett and was riding his bicycle down Winchester Road when he was run over by a motor car driven by Allan Douglas Hickman.

James Ashbolt was a passenger in the car and he testified that they had been travelling towards Shirley and as the vehicle approached the children's hospital a dark shape appeared as if from nowhere. The driver slammed on the brakes but couldn't help hitting whatever it was. It transpired that the dark shape was Douglas Jones and they had just run him over.

Marjorie May Jeans was walking along Winchester Road when Mr Jones came level with her, on his bicycle. Suddenly he gave a weird sounding cry, began to wobble and drift out into the centre of the road and fell off onto the tarmac. It was then that the car ran over him and she believed there was no way that the driver could have avoided the collision.

The dead man's father gave evidence that his son suffered epileptic fits and this corresponded with the evidence of Dr H. Castle who had performed the post-mortem. He told the court that the cause of death was shock following a fractured skull. It was his belief that Mr Jones had suffered a seizure, fallen off his bike, cracked his skull on the road and then been run over. It was his opinion that the poor man was dead even before the car hit him and no blame should be attached to the driver, Mr Hickman.

The coroner agreed with this scenario and returned a verdict of accidental death. He too stated that Mr Hickman was not at fault.

In the middle of October, another court case, this time concerning an illicit still, was brought before the magistrates at the Southampton Police Court.

John Leslie Courtney Coles of The Park, Naish Farm, New Milton appeared to answer seven separate summonses. The various summonses referred to the hawking of spirits at various locations between 24 March and 20 August 1942. The charges related to attempting to defraud the excise of duty on eight bottles of spirits, delivering 1½ litres of spirits without a permit and to distilling spirits without a licence at Pindi Farm, also in New Milton.

Mr Ryves, the solicitor for His Majesty's Customs and Excise, stated that the case had arisen due to a raid on a club. Bottles of spirits were found and it was determined that they had been distilled illicitly. The liquid in the bottles had a curious smell, similar to old rope. The spirits were rather crude and fiery and would not do a person much good if drunk in quantity.

The suggestion was that the defendant had gone around various premises selling his bottles of spirit. The purchasers gave a description of the man they had bought the bottles from and eventually he was spotted at New Milton. He was arrested and later his premises were searched and distilling apparatus was discovered.

Some of the landlords who had bought spirits from Coles were called to give evidence. For instance, Stanley Reginald Hughes, the licensee of the Cambridge Inn on Brinton's Road, said that Coles had visited him in April and offered some bottles of whisky. Coles did not admit that he had made the spirits himself but said that he had bought them cheaply in Edinburgh. Another witness said that he had purchased bottles of gin and whisky at £1 a bottle. All the landlords were shown a picture of Coles and all agreed that this was the man they had bought spirits from. Found guilty on all counts, Coles was fined £120 and a further 10 guineas in costs.

The same month of October saw the lowering of the conscription age to just 18 and on the very next day, 23 October, the Second Battle of El Alamein opened with a massive bombardment of the German positions. This was followed by an advance of the Australian forces who were supported by the Royal Navy on their right flank. The battle continued until 3 November and ended in a German retreat. Two days later, the milk ration in Britain was reduced to 2½ pints per week. Five days after that, though again it was not publicised at the time, British sailors boarded *U559* as it was sinking and retrieved another 'Enigma' machine and German code books.

In early November Florence Silvester of Lime Kiln Lane, Fawley, appeared in court at Southampton charged with ringing a bell. Florence had been summonsed for being a passenger in a public service vehicle in Waterloo Road, on 25 August, and ringing the bell for the vehicle to start.

The Deputy Town Clerk explained to the court that it was legal and a common practice for passengers to ring the bell in order to stop a bus but that it was illegal to do so in order to start the bus. Richard Wellstead, the bus driver, testified that he had stopped in Waterloo Road when the bell rang, presumably pushed by a passenger who wished to get off. The bell rang for a second time and he set off slowly but there was a cry from the passengers and a third ring so he stopped again. The bus conductress explained that she was upstairs at the time, collecting fares and was just about to ring the bell when the bus started up, someone else having rung the bell.

The problem was that the second bell ring had caused the driver to set off and one of the passengers getting off was thrown to the floor. Mrs Silvester denied that it was she who pushed the bell but other passengers said they had seen her do so. Found guilty, she was then fined 20s. and 14s. in costs.

November also saw more Allied success in North Africa. A major British offensive led to the capture of Tobruk on the 13th, and Benghazi on the 20th. It was this that led Churchill to make his famous comment, 'This is not the end. It is not even the beginning of the end. But it is, perhaps, the end of the beginning.'

At the end of the second week of December, one Southampton family received some great news when they discovered that their son, Flight Sergeant Francis Owen of Cawte Road, was a prisoner of war.

Originally, Francis had been reported missing but now the International Red Cross had been informed, through the German authorities, that he had been badly injured in the right leg but was alive and

Even in the dark days of 1942, Santa could still visit the local children in hospital.

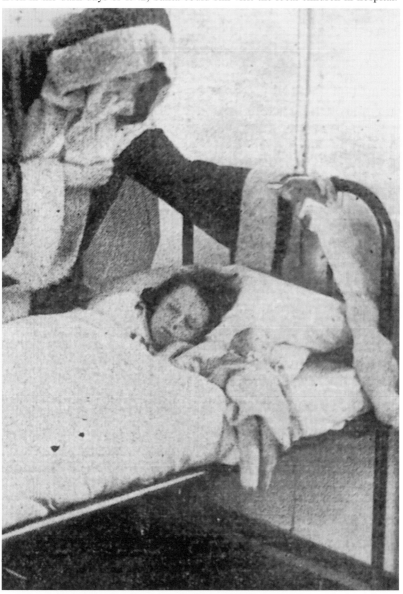

being looked after. Francis had also been promoted to pilot officer. The report in the *Echo* stated that Francis had been called up two days before the outbreak of the war, had been an air-gunner and wireless operator and had taken part in many raids over Germany and enemy occupied countries. He had been the rear gunner on an operation in September when his plane was hit several times and caught fire. Francis then had to bail out and was captured on landing.

CHAPTER SIX

1943

The year 1943 opened with a ban on civilians travelling to the Isle of Wight. This order would remain in force until 25 August 1944.

It could well be argued that the tide of the war began to turn in January 1943. On the 10th of the month, Soviet troops launched an all-out attack around Stalingrad. This resulted, on the 21st, in the capture of the last German airfield in the area meaning that they would no longer be able to re-supply their troops by air. The German forces in the region, led by General Friedrich Paulus, were now surrounded and cut off. Hitler ordered that they should not surrender and promoted Paulus to Field Marshal. Nevertheless, Paulus and the 6th Army did surrender on the last day of the month. Meanwhile, on 23 January, the British in North Africa captured Tripoli.

In Southampton there was quite a bad crash in The Avenue on 2 January when a bus collided with a tram. The bus was very badly damaged but fortunately there were no serious injuries, though a number of people had to be treated for shock, cuts and bruises.

Rationing was biting and there were many suggestions on how to eke out supplies.

The damage to the bus after it hit the tram in The Avenue in January 1943.

Salvage was important. This particular collection consists of aluminium utensils.

During the middle of the month the town received a visit from Herbert Morrison, the Minister for Home Security, who inspected members of the National Fire Service.

The Allied victories continued throughout February. At the beginning of the month Rommel retreated further into Tunisia and by the 5th, all of Libya was under Allied control. On the 9th of the month the Americans finally secured all of Guadalcanal.

Herbert Morrison on his visit to Southampton in January 1943.

On 4 March, an important case came before Southampton magistrates. A 17-year-old labourer, Cyril Charles Lakeland, of 8 Hazelbury Road, Totton, was facing a charge of murdering 79-year-old George Abrahams, of York Street, Northam, on 23 February.

At a previous hearing, Lakeland had been charged with causing grievous bodily harm, but on 25 February Abrahams, who had been employed as a firewatcher at the offices of the General Accident Fire and Life Assurance Corporation, had died from his injuries. The accused man, Lakeland, only had one hand, his left hand having been amputated some years before after an accident on the railway.

At the opening of the case Mr H.P. Roe, the deputy town clerk, outlined the case for the prosecution. For some time, Lakeland had been contemplating breaking into the company offices in Cumberland Place and he finally made his mind up to carry out his plan on 23 February. He told his girlfriend, Amy Kathleen Lane, what he intended to do and met her at some time between 4.30pm and 5.00pm on the fateful day.

The couple then went to Amy's sister's house at 22 Elgin Road for tea and it was here that Lakeland told four other people what he intended to do. There was an army bayonet in the sister's house and when Lakeland left at about 7.30pm, he took the weapon with him.

He and Amy then walked to Cumberland Place and upon arrival at the offices, Lakeland told his girlfriend to stay outside whilst he went in and robbed the place. Apparently, Lakeland knew that the back door of the premises was always left open so that the firewatchers could gain access to the building and he entered that way. Almost as soon as he had entered, he was approached by the firewatcher, George Abrahams, who he then struck over the head with the handle end of the bayonet. The end of the guard stick on the bayonet penetrated Abrahams's skull and he fell to the floor. Seeing this, Lakeland lost his nerve, dropped the bayonet and ran out of the building. They went back to the sister's house for more tea, where Lakeland washed blood off his hands before going home.

In due course, Lakeland was arrested and denied all knowledge of the crime. He made a statement to the police giving details of his supposed movements on the night in question but, when told by an officer that his timetable would have to be verified, Lakeland had apparently replied, 'You win, I did it.' He then made a second statement before being charged.

Both of Lakeland's statements were read out in court. In the second one he stated,

> Four months ago I had a friend who worked in an insurance office in Cumberland Place, next to the Royal Hotel. He told me that every night they left the keys of a safe in the right-hand drawer of a desk by the front window on the ground floor. He wanted me to go with him after office hours and rob the place.
>
> Even though I was short of money, owing to an accident on the railway which caused the loss of my left hand, I declined his offer. But on the 23rd of the month I was in debt and I wanted money badly, so I thought I would go to the insurance office.
>
> When I left Elgin Road with Miss Lane, I had in my possession a small case and a bayonet which belonged to the husband of Miss Lane's sister. I took this to open the drawer in case it was locked.
>
> I proceeded to the insurance office with Miss Lane. Arriving at the building at approximately 7.50pm, I went round the back, leaving Miss Lane outside on the pavement.
>
> I entered the back door and was about to go to the desk when I saw a firewatcher. I went back to the door and knocked on it very hard. I then hid underneath the stairs by the back door. The

firewatcher came and went outside with a torch. I was going towards the desk while he was out, but then he came back. I hid behind the wall, hoping he wouldn't see me. As he came past something came over me, and I hit him on the head with the hilt of the bayonet.

When I saw blood I lost my nerve, dropped the bayonet and ran out the way I had entered.

This morning, at work, I burnt a handkerchief, which was covered with blood. I burnt it on an electric fire and scattered the ashes on some waste ground outside the factory.

Witnesses were then called to add further evidence. Dr John Stewart Seaton stated that when Mr Abrahams was brought into the hospital he was unconscious, and suffering from a depressed fracture of the frontal area of the skull. An operation was performed and several pieces of bone were removed from the injured man's brain. He died at 6.10pm on the 25th, without ever regaining consciousness.

Herbert William Spain was another firewatcher on the premises where the crime took place. He stated that when Abrahams had arrived for work he had been in good spirits. At some time, close to 8.00pm he heard someone calling and, looking out of a window, he saw Abrahams staggering about near the back door, crying out for help. Going to his colleague's assistance, Spain had administered first aid and called for the police and an ambulance. Later he found the bayonet under a desk in the office.

Lakeland's girlfriend, Amy, said she had known the prisoner for about eight years and they had been engaged since the previous October. She then confirmed the movements outlined in Lakeland's statement adding that she had tried to dissuade him from his intended course of action. After hearing all the evidence, the magistrates ordered that Lakeland be sent for trial on the charge of murder.

Lakeland's trial opened on 1 April at the Central Criminal Court in London. After hearing all the evidence, the jury decided that he was guilty as charged. He was, of course, too young to hang so the judge had no option but to sentence him to be detained until His Majesty's Pleasure be known.

On the first day of May, Southampton magistrates sent Stanley McAllen, a scrap-metal dealer, to jail for one month for failing to comply with a directive to take employment as a trainee on munitions work. The directive had been given by the national service officer on about 14 December 1942 but McAllen had ignored it. This was the second time he had appeared in court to answer the charge, having pleaded not guilty at the first in March.

At the end of the first week of May, the Mayor, Councillor Corry, started a 'Mile of Pennies' appeal on behalf of the Royal South Hants and Southampton Hospital. The main collecting point was the forecourt of the Southampton gas company showrooms. The Mayor and Mayoress were greeted by Alderman Wooley, the chairman of the management committee at the hospital, and the matron, Miss Smith.

Nurses from the hospital formed a guard of honour at the event and the Mayor was presented with a buttonhole and his wife a spray of carnations, by nurses Wilkie and Parkinson. The Mayor made a speech urging people to donate and said he hoped they would raise more money than the previous year, which had raised £1,119.

There was another boost for Allied morale in mid-May with news of Operation Chastise, the bombing of the German dams in the Ruhr valley. This had been carried out by 617 Squadron of the RAF which used bouncing bombs to hit the targets, the raid taking place over the evening of 16/17 May.

A remarkable coincidence was reported at the end of May. Three cousins, all from Canada, were all serving in the armed forces. Private Eric Cooper, Private Thomas Palser and Sergeant Milton Blackwood lived many miles from each other back in Canada and, as a consequence, they had never met each other. Neither had they ever met their aunt, Mrs Norman, who lived at 45 Cedar Road, but all three independently decided to visit her on the same day and arrived at the house within hours of each other.

Fortunately, Mrs Norman was a trained cook and managed to eke out the three mutton chops she had intended to serve up for herself and her daughter, Doris. The boys were provided with an excellent meal which ended with a delightful cake, also cooked by Mrs Norman.

Tunis was captured by the British First Army on 7 May. Six days later, on the 13th, the remaining Afrika Korps and Italian troops in North Africa surrendered to the Allies. Over 250,000 prisoners were taken.

On 4 June, Herbert Charles William Street, a deaf and dumb Southampton ARP warden, was awarded the BEM in the King's birthday honours. Mr Street was also a sergeant in the Home Guard and was given the award in recognition of his admirable services to civil defence and for training other deaf and dumb people in the ARP.

He was also involved in heroic fire-fighting duties during raids on the town. His colleagues were delighted that Herbert had been honoured.

Herbert had enrolled in civil defence in June 1938, whilst working as a draughtsman at the Ordnance Survey office, but was seconded to a war factory soon after hostilities were delcared. Herbert explained that he knew when planes were overheard despite being totally deaf by holding a piece of metal in his hand through which he could feel vibrations, and when the sirens went off he was woken up by his dog, which slept under his bed.

The good news continued in July. Palermo in Sicily was captured by American troops commanded by General Patton. Three days later Benito Mussolini was arrested and relieved of his offices after a meeting with King Victor Emmanuel III. Marshal Pietro Badoglio was asked to form a new government.

In was also in July that the *Echo* carried a story about a new facility designed especially for the American allies, a home from home in the form of the American Red Cross Service clubs.

One such club was situated on the south side of Bargate, which one user said gave him acute nostalgia. There were two other clubs, one in Above Bar and one on Portland Street. The clubs all sported the sort of welcome sign that featured at the edge of every township in the US and all had a register, so that men could check to see if anyone from their home town was there.

There were large, comfortable recreation rooms furnished with big armchairs and rugs, which could easily be rolled to allow for dancing.

How Trafalgar Day was publicised in 1943, to rally the 'Bulldog' spirit.

Upstairs was a restaurant worthy of five stars where British chefs produced pure American cuisine. A doughnut-making plant was expected to open soon.

On 12 August, Hedge End baker Frederick Watts was fined £2 for selling a loaf of bread not being one full pound in weight. The offence had taken place on 27 July and in court Watts explained that he had been in business for twenty years and this was the first time his bread had been underweight. That defence was somewhat negated by evidence that on the day in question, thirty-three loaves had been tested and seven of them were found to be underweight.

At the beginning of September, Southampton magistrates imposed a three-month prison sentence on a 'witness'. Daphne Lila Jays, of Bridlington Avenue, Shirley was found guilty of failing to comply with the conditions on which she registered as a conscientious objector on 17 July, namely that she should undertake full-time work as either a hospital worker or land worker. She had pleaded not guilty to the charge, claiming that she had a reasonable excuse for not obeying the order. Daphne was a Jehovah's Witness and had made a statement in which she said that her course of action was dictated solely by a desire to obey God's commands. That was not enough for the magistrates who, as stated, imposed the prison sentence.

The country at large had something to celebrate in September when it was announced that Italy had surrendered and had dropped out of the war. A secret armistice had been signed on 3 September but it was only officially announced by President Roosevelt on the 8th. This did not, however, lead to the end of hostilities in Italy because the German forces disarmed the Italians and took over the defence of the country. The Allies would be forced to fight their way up through Italy, after landing at Salerno on 9 September.

It was also in September that German SS troops rescued Mussolini from captivity. The following month, on 13 October, Italy declared war on Germany. Italian troops would now fight against men who had recently been their allies.

The town had another regal visitor on 4 September when the Princess Royal, Commander in Chief of the British Red Cross Society, visited to inspect various Red Cross activities. The princess said she was much impressed by the efficiency of all the work in the town. A parade of over 600 officers and members was the highlight of the day.

There was news that a consignment of oranges from South Africa was due to arrive in Southampton on 10 November. Also expected was a small consignment of lemons from Sicily. This fruit, however, was not for general public consumption but would be distributed through the NAAFI to the crews of submarines and to airmen engaged in operational duties.

It was also in November, on the 28th, that a conference took place in Tehran between Roosevelt, Churchill and Stalin at which it was agreed that an Allied invasion of mainland Europe would take place in June 1944, though no official date was set. It would be codenamed Operation Overlord.

The year ended with some sad statistics showing that it had been a black Christmas on Southampton's roads. There had been three fatalities, all during the blackout on Christmas Eve, bringing the total number of deaths for the year to eighteen. Charles James Bailey, 51, a milk roundsman of 17 Dorset Street, William Lomax, 60, a labourer of the Salvation Army Hostel, Bond Street, Northam, and Alfred Prior, 67, a pensioner of 8 St Michael's Square, were the three men who lost their lives during the festive season.

CHAPTER SEVEN

1944

The year 1944 began with the Red Army entering Poland and at the end of January, the RAF dropped 2,300 tons of bombs on Berlin. The war was now being taken back to Germany.

February saw the destruction of the Benedictine monastery on Monte Cassino, but also the Germans launched a major attack on the beachhead at Anzio, threatening the American forces there.

March held a mixture of good and bad news for the Allies. The German assault on Anzio failed but on the 7th, Japanese forces finally attacked India and a major battle began around Imphal. Meanwhile, back in Britain, a rather archaic law was wiped off the statute books. Married women could now work as teachers.

On the 18th, the Red Army approached the Romanian frontier but the very next day German forces occupied Hungary in order to protect their ally from the Russian advances. Meanwhile, the Japanese began to advance all along the Imphal front. It seemed that a breaking point must come soon in the various theatres of war.

At the beginning of May, the Southampton Borough Coroner, Mr Arthur Emanuel, presided over a tragic case involving the death of a young soldier, Vernon Howard Symons. Evidence given by Major Clayton Edward Fuller showed that a group of soldiers were engaged on a training exercise showing the correct use of an explosive. The men were all lying down 30yds away from the site of the explosion, and all were wearing their steel helmets. The device was detonated and Symons was found to be injured. It appeared that a large piece of shrapnel had struck him in the face, causing extensive injuries. Symons was rushed to hospital where he was seen by Dr G.W. Barker, but found to be dead on arrival. His injuries included a fractured skull. The coroner returned a verdict of accidental death pointing out, 'At times like these all sorts of dangers have to be incurred.'

It was also in May that a new Southampton industry was publicised. It seemed that the increase in taxation on tobacco products meant that many smokers could no longer afford to fund their habit. Some entrepreneurial individuals had taken to waiting for the cleaners outside busy establishments such as the local cinemas. When the bins were brought out these men would carefully sift through the wrappers and cartons in search of old cigarette ends. These they would collect, carefully cut off the ends and the paper and store the remaining tobacco in jars. They would then use this free tobacco to fill their own pipes and to roll their own new cigarettes. However, the more successful of them would also have tobacco left over which they would then sell to their friends, thus funding a night out in the local pub.

In the same month the invasion of German-occupied Europe and the setting up of a western front was timetabled for 5 June. Later in the month, on the 18th, Monte Cassino was finally captured by Polish troops. Finally, on the last day of May, the Japanese retreated from Imphal and their invasion of India came to an end.

The planned invasion of 5 June had to be put back to 6 June as a result of bad weather. A total of 155,000 men landed on the beaches of Normandy. A second front had now been opened up in Europe. Two days before this, on 4 June, Allied troops had occupied Rome after the Germans had declared it an open city. Later, on 13 June, Hitler launched the first of his new revenge weapons, the V1, against England. Eight civilians were killed by that first bomb and further attacks would be made throughout the month.

In July, readers of the *Echo* were told of a fortuitous meeting somewhere in Italy. Private Charles Hunt, of 22 Milner Street, Shirley, was at a rest camp in Italy wondering if his brother, Gunner George Hunt, was alive and well. No sooner had he picked up pencil and paper but George walked into the tent. He had been sent to the same rest camp.

In his letter home, Charles wrote, 'You will be surprised to know I have been with George for a week at the rest camp. On arrival I made enquiries about his regiment when lo and behold, on looking up there was George.' Before joining the army, Charles had been in the building trade whilst his brother had worked for the Southern Railway at Southampton docks.

It was also in July that an attempt was made to assassinate Hitler and bring the war to an end. On the 20th, Colonel Claus von Stauffenberg planted a bomb close to Hitler during a meeting at Rastenburg in East Prussia. Hitler survived the blast and terrible reprisals followed against those accused of being involved. It was even suggested that Field Marshal Rommel was one of the conspirators, but he avoided the initial investigations as he had been seriously wounded on the 17th when his car was machine-gunned from the air.

The Warsaw Uprising began on 1 August, with the Polish people believing that help would soon come from the ever advancing Russian forces. That help never came and the heroic actions of the Poles ended in tragedy.

In the same month of August, the 170th competition for the 'Knighthood' of the old bowling green was held. This was attended by a number of local dignitaries including the Mayor and his wife. Also present was Mr William Day, the senior 'Knight'.

The V1, or 'Doodlebug', attacks continued over the capital. The 12 August marked the sixtieth day of the campaign and the bombs claimed the lives of more than 6,000 people, with a further 17,000 injured.

Another Axis power was knocked out of the war on 23 August when Romania surrendered to the Russians and immediately joined the Allied side. By the end of the month two more previously occupied capital cities were liberated. The first was Paris, freed from occupation on the 25th. The second was Bucharest, liberated by Russian troops on the last day of the month.

The good news continued into September with the Allied invasion of Belgium and the freeing of yet another capital city, Brussels, on 3 September. This time the liberating troops were British in the form of the Second Army.

On 9 September, another new weapon was unleashed onto the people of Britain when the first V2 rocket landed in London. It struck in the Chiswick area and killed three people, but the very next day the first small portion of Germany itself was taken by the Allies when they captured Aachen.

Meanwhile, in Southampton, news was received that Sapper William Charles Harry Hibberd, who lived in Glenfield Crescent, Bitterne, had been killed in action in north-west Europe. Hibberd, who had been a bulldozer driver in the Royal Engineers, had worked for the Pirelli General Cable Company in civilian life, and was an only son.

At the beginning of October, at the county court before Judge Topham, a case for compensation opened. Rosaline Eliza Atkinson of Willis Road, Swaythling, was claiming damages against 19-year-old Peter Jenkins, a student at University College. The proceedings related to an accident that had taken place at a tram stop in Burgess Road, on 16 May. Rosaline was waiting to board a tram and she now claimed that Peter's negligence, whilst riding a bicycle, had caused her to suffer injuries.

Giving her evidence, Rosaline explained that at about 4.40pm on the day in question she intended to catch the tram. She looked both right and left, saw nothing coming, and so stepped out towards the tram. She stood back a little way in order to allow passengers to alight and caught sight of something out of the corner of her eye before everything went blank.

As a result of the collision with the bicycle of Mr Jenkins she was in hospital for ten days and continued to receive medical treatment until the end of June. Her injuries were mainly on the right side of her body and included a fracture of her clavicle and a deep cut to her head.

Reginald McCarra, a customs officer, had witnessed the accident. He testified that he saw the plaintiff standing about 18in from the tram and slightly to the rear of it. He saw the cyclist come from the middle of the road and attempt to pass between Miss Atkinson and the tram. The defendant stated that he did not see Miss Atkinson until the last moment and tried to swerve in order to avoid her.

The trial judge stated that because of his hesitation the accident was the cyclist's fault and he awarded compensation and costs totalling £89.11s. He also commented that it was unfortunate that Southampton was one of the few towns that persisted in running its trams in the middle part of the road. This was a most dangerous form of locomotion and it often caused people, cyclists and even motor cars to attempt to overtake the trams on the near side which was very dangerous indeed.

The ill-fated Warsaw Uprising was finally crushed on 2 October but another capital city, Athens, was liberated on the 12th. Two days after this, on the 14th, Rommel took his own life in order to save his family from any possible retributions against them after the bomb plot against Hitler. Rommel was subsequently buried with full military honours.

In mid-October Southampton welcomed the arrival of a true war hero in the form of Private A.G. Gordon, who was home on leave after returning from the ill-fated attack upon Arnhem. Private Gordon was now living in Winchester, although he was a native of Southampton, the reason being that his real home in the town had been destroyed by German bombing. He had originally joined the army in March 1940 and since then had fought in no less than seven campaigns including the Western Desert, Syria, Burma, Sicily and Italy. Throughout all that heavy fighting he hadn't sustained as much as a scratch, though he had seen comrades perish and had actually buried one of his friends himself, after he had been killed in North Africa. Asked by a reporter what had impressed him most, he replied, with a cheeky smile, 'Having dinner in England after we had breakfasted in France.'

President Roosevelt won an unprecedented fourth term in office on 6 November.

On a more local note, on Thursday, 9 November, the borough council debated the idea of Southampton becoming a holiday resort after the war was over. Amongst the points discussed were that the corporation should sell the advertising space on their buses and trams direct to advertisers, through an advertising manager. In addition, a study should be made of the archaeological and antiquarian points of interest within the town and its environs and that there should be guided tours of the areas relating to the ancient British people, Saxons, Romans and Normans. Another suggestion was that licences should be issued to authorised guides.

This would mean that there should be an expansion of suitable accommodation incorporating new hotels, hostels and boarding houses. Further, once a plan of action had been formalised, it should involve various outside bodies including the Harbour Board, the Chamber of Commerce, Southern Railway, the Isle of Wight Steam Packet Company and other omnibus companies.

Towards the end of the month of November, Hitler left his headquarters at Rastenberg and returned to Berlin. Once there he established himself in the bunker where he would remain for the rest of the war. In the same month, on the 25th, a V2 bomb struck a Woolworth's store in south-east London, killing 168 people. It was the costliest V2 attack of the entire war.

An inquest on 11 December considered the death of Sydney Stanley Fullerton of 110 Bevois Street, who had been fatally injured on 4 December when his bicycle was involved in a collision with a truck in Millbrook Road. Corporal Jeremiah Clancy, who was a passenger in the truck, stated that they were driving along Millbrook Road, heading in the direction of Totton. The road was entirely clear, apart from a man on a bicycle. As the truck drew level with the bicycle, Mr Fullerton, for no apparent reason, turned towards the truck. The driver, Leading Aircraftman Cecil Douglas Jeffrey, a native of Aldershot, shouted a warning and tried to turn the truck but it was to no avail. There was a loud bang, Jeffrey stopped the truck and found that he had struck the cyclist.

Doctor Bartecek had taken care of the injured man at the hospital but he succumbed to his injuries on 7 December. A post-mortem examination showed that Mr Fullerton had sustained a fractured skull and lacerations of the brain. The Deputy Borough Coroner, Mr D.H.B. Harfield, returned a verdict of accidental death and expressed his deepest sympathies to the dead man's mother, Annie.

A terrible fire in Bernard Street in December claimed the lives of two beautiful children, the eldest of which was most probably the cause of the conflagration. Grace Banfield lived at 95 Bernard Road with her mother, Mrs Kay, and her two children, 3-year-old Mavis Christine and 9-month-old Joan Kathleen. Their father, Albert James Banfield, was away from home, serving in the Merchant Navy.

At about 6.15pm on Wednesday, 22 December Mrs Banfield put the two girls to bed in separate cots. Their bedroom was at the back on the ground floor. At about 8.15pm Grace heard a noise coming from upstairs and upon going to investigate, found Mavis, naked, sitting on the floor and scribbling on a writing pad with a pencil. She explained that she was writing a letter to daddy. Mavis was in the habit of removing her nightclothes, preferring to sleep without them. It was something she had done before. With a gentle admonishment, Grace put her daughter's nightdress back on and put her back into her cot.

Everything remained quiet until 9.15pm when Grace's mother, Mrs Kay, said that she had heard something upstairs. Grace again went to investigate and found, to her horror, that the children's bedroom was ablaze. Quickly she picked up Joan from her cot, which was the closest one, and took her down to the basement. She then went back to the bedroom to try to save Mavis but the flames were too much now. Grace tried her best but she was beaten back sustaining burns to her hands, arms and face in the process.

The fire was eventually brought under control by the fire service and Mavis's body was recovered. Joan too subsequently perished and when Dr A.W. Banks performed post-mortems on both of the children's bodies he reported that both had sustained burns. Mavis had died from shock as a direct result of extensive burns. Joan had

The result of the terrible fire in Bernard Street in December 1944.

died from asphyxiation, caused by the smoke, but she too had suffered charring and burns.

The inquest into the tragedy took place on 23 December by which time the girl's father, Albert, had been given special leave to attend the hearing. After Grace had told her story and Dr Banks had given his evidence, James Alfred Caws, a fireman, gave his testimony. He stated that a piece of blue woollen material had been found, charred and burned, on top of the fireguard in the room.

Grace Banfield had already told the court that on the night in question there had been a fire in the grate in the children's bedroom. When the girls were put to bed the fire was almost out and there was a fireguard in front of it. There was no clothing or anything else on that guard. She was also able to say that Mavis had a blue woollen dressing gown.

Mavis Banfield, one of the children who perished in the Bernard Street fire.

In his summing up, the coroner said that the evidence showed that it was almost certain that what had happened was that Mavis, who had already taken her nightdress off earlier that night, had, in all probability, got up again and put her dressing gown over the fire-guard herself. That had caught fire, resulting in the tragedy. No blame should be attached to the mother and this was clearly an accident.

It was also in December that the Home Guard was stood down. The Axis powers in Europe were collapsing and there was no longer the slightest chance that any invasion of Britain would be mounted by the Germans. There was, however, an attempt by Hitler to retake Antwerp by launching the Battle of the Bulge. Initial successes by the Germans would be pushed back by the Americans. It seemed that the end might finally be in sight. The New Year held a great deal of promise.

The Armistice Day wreath-laying in 1944.

CHAPTER EIGHT

An Accusation of Murder

On 29 January 1945, a mother and daughter faced a murder charge at Southampton. Joyce Smith, 20, and her mother, Nora Petcher, 45, both of 23 Janson Road, Shirley, were accused of the murder of Joyce's baby, Raymond John Smith, who was aged just 7 months at the time of his death. The baby, it seemed, was an unwanted child who during his short life was looked after by a number of foster mothers.

Raymond had been born in the Borough Hospital at Southampton on 15 May 1944 and left the hospital on 27 May in the care of Mrs Florence May Behan, a relative of the two accused, by marriage; her sister had married Nora Petcher's son. She kept the child until September, at her home in South Wales. After her circumstances changed, she found she could no longer look after the boy and asked Joyce Smith, the mother, to take him back. When faced with this request, Joyce threatened to simply abandon her son and even suggested that Mrs Behan should leave him on a train for someone else to pick up.

On 23 September Raymond was taken into hospital as an abandoned child. He stayed there until 26 September when he was given into the care of Mrs Ethel Renee Eade, of Cobden Gardens, Southampton, another foster mother who said she would be happy to look after him.

Unfortunately, Raymond was only able to stay with Mrs Eade until November when she was advised, on medical grounds, to hand him back to his mother. On 16 November her husband, Albert Edward Eade, took Raymond back to 23 Janson Road but was unable to hand him over to either Joyce or Nora. Mr Eade was forced to leave him with Mrs Gwendoline Mona Tiller, who rented a room in the same house.

It became clear that Raymond's mother did not want him back. When Mrs Tiller tried to hand him over Joyce flatly refused to have him and on one occasion said to Mrs Tiller, 'I don't want the child back here. If it comes back I will get rid of it by hook or by crook.'

Later, when Mrs Tiller said that looking after the child was getting too much for her, she repeated that she had to hand Raymond back. Nora Petcher replied, 'Then I shall have to put it to sleep.' Later still, at 9.30am on 4 December, Mrs Tiller saw Joyce Smith breaking up some tablets and crushing them in a milk jug. Seeing that Mrs Tiller was watching her, she commented, 'I am going to put them in the baby's bottle to put him to sleep.' Later the same day, at about 3.30pm, Mrs Tiller asked after the baby's health and Joyce said that he was dead. Nora said, 'We will bury it in the garden.' Joyce then replied, 'No, I think I would rather burn the body. I'm afraid the dog might smell it if it is buried, and dig it up.' In fact, the child's body was both buried and burned and was finally found in a garden shed at the back of 23 Janson Road, in a bath, covered with earth and the whole thing covered with a dressing gown.

The following day, 5 December, Mrs Tiller noticed that the dustbin had been moved close to the window of her room. She asked Joyce and Nora what the bin was doing there and Nora replied that they were going to use it to burn Raymond's body. Mrs Tiller asked them to move the bin, which they did. Later she saw Nora Petcher but a cardboard box into the bin. Joyce Smith then poured paraffin into the bin and set a match to it. There was a big fire, a lot of smoke and an awful smell. Mrs Tiller had to leave the house and when she returned, the two defendants were digging a hole in the garden.

On New Year's Eve, 31 December 1944, police officers asking after the child went to the house and spoke to both women. Nora claimed that Raymond had been adopted and Joyce confirmed this, adding, 'Oh yes, someone up north has adopted it.' However, they had told other stories to neighbours and friends who had also asked after the boy. Under questioning, Joyce finally said that she had given Raymond two sleeping tablets in his milk as he would not settle at night. She had a good night's sleep for the first time but on waking the following morning she found that her son was dead. She did not know what to do so put him in a box and buried him in the garden. Later she dug him up again and put him in the bath with the soil.

When Nora was questioned she placed all the blame squarely on Joyce's shoulders. She claimed that Joyce had not let her have anything to do with the disposal of the body. She added that Joyce had told her that she had given Raymond aspirin and it had killed him.

The body of the baby had been handed over to Professor Webster on 2 January 1945. He had made an examination and concluded that death was due to aspirin poisoning.

On the second day of the magistrate's court hearing no less than five doctors were called to give evidence. The first of those witnesses was Dr Maurice Kirkpatrick Jardine, the medical superintendent at the Borough Hospital, who confirmed that Joyce Smith had been admitted to the hospital on 15 May 1944, and gave birth to her son on the same day. He also confirmed that she was discharged from the hospital on 27 May. The child was readmitted, through the action of the police, on 23 September as a stranded child and remained there until the 26th.

Dr David Parr Lockhart said that on 30 November 1944 Mrs Eade brought Raymond to his surgery. The child was suffering from infant eczema and a scabies infection. He advised her to return the baby to its mother.

Dr Francis Joseph Eager, a dermatologist at the Royal South Hants and Southampton Hospital, gave evidence that on 15 November Raymond was brought to the hospital, suffering from eczema. He treated the child, which was otherwise perfectly healthy at the time.

The next doctor to take the stand was Dr Alan George Raine Whitehouse of the West Midlands Forensic Science Laboratory at Birmingham who had examined a number of organs taken from the child's body. This revealed the presence of 2.47 grains of aspirin.

Dr James Webster reported his findings after carrying out a post-mortem on the dead child. He had made his examination on 2 January 1945 and concluded that Raymond had been dead for between four and six weeks. The body had been badly damaged by fire but the child had been dead when it was put onto the fire. He had heard Dr Whitehouse's evidence and concurred that the cause of death was aspirin poisoning.

Mrs Behan explained that she lived in Wallington in Surrey but in April 1944 she was staying at 23 Janson Road after being bombed out of her London home. She testified that she had taken care of Raymond when he was brought home from the hospital. She had wanted to adopt the child and Joyce was happy for her to do so but she discovered that she was unable to do so as she was under 25 years of age.

After returning to London with the baby, and then, because of the continued bombing, moving to South Wales, she obtained full-time work at a Royal Ordnance factory and could no longer devote enough time to Raymond, so she took him back to Southampton. When she told the two defendants that she should have to return the boy, they flew into a temper and even locked her in one of the rooms for over half an hour. After much argument she returned to Wales with Raymond but took him back again on 23 September. Unable to get to speak to either Joyce or Nora, she was forced to take the baby to the police and they arranged for him to be admitted to the hospital.

After hearing all this evidence, the magistrates decided that both women should be sent for trial on a charge of wilful murder. That trial opened, before Mr Justice Tucker, at Winchester, on 6 March 1945 and lasted for four days. The case for the prosecution was led by Mr G.D. Roberts, assisted by Mr F.S. Laskey. Joyce Smith was defended by Mr N.R. Fox-Andrews assisted by Mr A.C. Munro Kerr. Nora Petcher was represented by Mr J. Scott Henderson and Mr Raymond Stock. The jury included two women.

At the opening of the trial the legal representatives of both of the accused made an application to have them tried separately. It was contended that there were a number of pieces of evidence against one prisoner that would be detrimental to the other if the two were tried together. Several previous cases were discussed including that of Thompson and Bywaters but Mr Justice Tucker ruled that the case should be heard as it stood adding that he did not see that there could be any possible miscarriage of justice.

The trial proper then began and other witnesses, in addition to those already detailed, gave evidence for the prosecution.

Detective Inspector Gordon Baker told the court of a visit he made to the prisoner's house on 31 December 1944 after Mrs Tiller had been to the police station and reported the disappearance of the child. He first spoke to Mrs Petcher and asked where the child was. She replied that he had been adopted. Soon afterwards, Mrs Smith entered the room and confirmed this, adding that the baby had been taken to the north of England. Both prisoners were then asked to make formal statements.

In her statement Joyce Smith said that the baby did not sleep at night and would not take any food. She claimed that she was so worried that she gave him two small sleeping tablets in his bottle. The next day he had passed away and she panicked and decided that she needed to dispose of the body. She had put him into a little box and was going to burn him but decided against that and buried him in the garden. Her uncle was about to visit, though, and she knew he would do some digging in the garden so she dug the body up and hid it in a bath. Later she made an addition to her statement in which she admitted that she did try to burn the body but it was getting dark and the flames would break the blackout regulations.

In her statement Nora Petcher said that Joyce would not allow her to have anything to do with the disposal of the child's body.

Superintendent William Turner told the court that he had attended the house in Janson Road with Detective Inspector Baker on 31 December and made a search of the premises. He found the small galvanised bath covered over and containing earth. He removed the bath to Shirley police station where it was examined. The badly charred body of the child was found in it. Some of the limbs were missing.

The case for the prosecution being completed, the defence case was now outlined. Joyce Smith stated that she was married, in 1941, at Weston-super-Mare. Her husband was in the forces and had the rank of leading aircraftman. The relationship did not last and they parted in 1942 but she was pregnant at the time and gave birth to a daughter in May 1943. Her husband never offered any financial support for his daughter and the child was looked after by Joyce's parents. After this, in order to support herself, she took a job as a welder for the Southern Railway. As for Raymond, his father had been an American merchant seaman she had had a brief relationship with.

Turning to the death of Raymond, Joyce tried to implicate Mrs Tiller stating that she had given her the tablets, seemed unemotional when informed of the baby's death and had then advised her on how to get rid of the body. In fact, Mrs Tiller had helped her to do so.

The time came for Nora Petcher to enter the witness box. She simply denied all the evidence given by Mrs Tiller. She had never suggested disposing of Raymond's body, had taken no part in it and knew nothing of it until Joyce told her what had happened and confessed that the baby was buried in the garden. It had been about the middle of December when Joyce spoke to her about the matter. Until then she had understood that the baby had been handed over to a convent.

The evidence having been heard and the summing up for the prosecution and defence having been made, Mr Justice Tucker made his final statements to the jury. He pointed out that if they should find the prisoners guilty of murder, Joyce Smith would not face the death penalty as she was pregnant again. The judge's summation lasted for a total of 2 hours and 25 minutes.

The jury retired to consider their verdict. After an hour they returned to court to ask for advice on the prescribing of tablets. Could a doctor give tablets that contained 12 grains of aspirin? The judge gave his opinion and the jury went back to their deliberations. After another 70 minutes they came back to court with their verdict. They found both prisoners not guilty of murder but guilty of manslaughter. Both women were then sentenced to three years' imprisonment. Both Nora and Joyce almost collapsed and had to be supported by the warders standing behind them.

CHAPTER NINE

The Cul-de-Sac Murder

At 8.15am on Tuesday, 13 February, Frederick George Edmunds of 139 Bellemore Road, Shirley, was walking to work along New Road. As he passed the end of Exmouth Street, a cul-de-sac, he saw the body of a woman lying on the ground. Frederick approached and seeing that the woman was dead, stopped a passing schoolboy, 16-year-old Peter Cecil Jeffries, and told him to run for the police. Peter wasted no time in doing as he had been asked.

By 10.00am, a canvas tent had been erected over the body. This was not just for the sake of public decency but because rain had fallen heavily overnight and there was the promise of more to come. It also enabled Dr Geoffrey Gordon Havers, the senior police surgeon, to make his initial examination.

The woman was lying on her back with her clothing disarranged. The lower part of her body was exposed and it seemed reasonable to assume that she had been raped. There were marks of injury around her face and neck, bruises on her legs and a superficial wound over her right knee where her stocking had been torn. The subsequent post-mortem, carried out by Professor J.M. Webster, at which Dr Havers assisted, would show that the cause of death was strangulation.

There was a curious factor to the case which, at least for the time being, the police kept back from the press and the general public. An army beret had been folded and placed beneath the woman's head. If this belonged to her killer, which seemed highly likely, it could prove to be a valuable clue.

Close by the body was a small, brown leather shopping bag and the contents of this would lead quickly to an identification of the victim. The dead woman was 55-year-old Mary Helen Hoyles, who preferred to be known by her middle name. She had been a kitchen worker at an American Red Cross Club in High Street and that was the next port of call for the police.

Mary Helen Hoyles, victim of the cul-de-sac murder.

Ernest Albert Williams was the assistant to the directors of the American Club and he would later make a positive identification of the victim. He told the police that Helen had worked at the club for around nine or ten months. She didn't work on the counter itself but would usually be employed making sandwiches in the room at the back. By speaking to other women who worked there, the police were able to confirm that Helen had worked at the club on the night of Monday, 12 February and had signed the time sheet upon leaving for the night. That showed she had left for home at 10.40pm that night.

An appeal was made, through the local newspapers, for anyone who had seen a woman matching Helen's description, after 10.40pm. The description given was, '5ft 4in in height. Medium build and medium brown hair. Wearing an imitation animal skin coat with a small American Red Cross badge pinned to the lapel. Wore a greenish coloured scarf around her neck. Also wearing a dark blue woollen frock. Stockings with low-heeled shoes with green uppers and yellow piping.'

A witness soon came forward to say that he had seen a woman fitting that description in Above Bar, with a soldier, shortly before 11.00pm. He could not say that they were actually in each other's company as Helen seemed to walking a little ahead. The soldier, who appeared to be the worse for drink, was a little behind. He did say something to Helen and she replied by turning her head and speaking over her shoulder. This did fit in with Helen's known regular movements. Whenever she left the club she was in the habit of walking straight up Above Bar until she turned down New Road. She rented two rooms at 40 New Road and would pass the end of Exmouth Street in order to get home.

A description of this soldier was now published. According to the witness who had seen him with Helen, he was, 'White, aged about 25

The Hoyles murder scene, 1945.

and about 5ft 8in tall. He was of average build with light hair and was wearing a light field jacket with a zip fastener. He also wore a cap.'

The inquest opened on Friday, 16 February. One of Helen's brothers, Harry Hoyles of Keyhaven, Hampshire, was present and he was able to give some detailed information about his sister's background. The Hoyles had originally been based in Lynton, North Devon and Helen had come from a very large family, there being seven sons and three daughters. Helen had left school at the age of 14 and immediately gone into service. Harry had not seen his sister again until 1916 by which time she was a waitress at a hotel in Halifax. The next time he saw her was at their mother's funeral, at Lynton, in 1929 by which time Helen had already moved to Southampton where she had started a poultry farm, but that venture had soon failed. By the summer of 1938 she had managed to set up a small general shop in New Road and he had visited her there.

Unfortunately, Helen's shop was destroyed in the Blitz towards the end of 1940 and a number of jobs followed in quick succession. Initially, she had worked for Oxborrow's Tyre Depot in New Road but soon left there to take up a job at the gasworks. From there she obtained a position in the pantry of the Royal Hotel in Cumberland Place before working at the Southern Railway canteen at the docks.

Her penultimate position was in the ARP canteen in the Civic Centre before she moved to the American Club in May 1944. Her ambition, apparently, was to save enough money to open a new shop, once the war was over.

Once evidence of identification and cause of death were given, the inquest was adjourned for six months, until 25 August, though the coroner did explain that it would be reopened immediately if the miscreant was arrested.

On 20 February a valuable new witness came forward. An American naval seaman stated that he had been with a young Southampton girl on the night of Monday, the 12th. At some time about 11.00pm they were passing the entrance to Exmouth Street when they heard a woman's voice coming from the cul-de-sac, saying in a muffled, pleading voice, 'Don't kill me, please, please.' They had not reported this because they thought it was just a couple skylarking and the American had gone to sea the following morning and had not heard about the murder until his return.

The couple also reported that, although they could not see a couple in the cul-de-sac, they did see an American soldier standing outside the Bay Tree Inn, which was on the corner of Exmouth Street. He was leaning with his back against the pub wall, and one leg bent back, the foot resting on the wall itself. For the first time the police had to consider that there might have been two men involved in the murder; one who acted as a look-out and one who committed the rape and murder.

The police now decided to release some further information which they had kept back until now. First, details and pictures of the cap found under Helen's head were released. Unfortunately, there was no insignia or name on the cap but hairs had been found inside and these might help in identifying the owner. They also gave details of another soldier they wished to trace. Helen did not work on Thursdays and was in the habit of visiting the Robert Burns public house on her evenings off. She had been seen there in the company of an American soldier described as being 35 to 40 years old, medium build, fair hair and with staring eyes.

Thought to be of more import were the results of a search of Helen's rooms which she rented from Miss Irene Adams. This revealed a number of letters and two in particular seemed to be of especial interest.

Although Helen, and other women, worked in the kitchen at the back of the club, they could be seen from the main rooms and it was the habit of some servicemen to write notes which they would hand to a barmaid who would pass them on to women in the kitchen. It seemed that these two notes might well have come into Helen's hands in this manner.

The first of these notes read, 'Dear You, What time may one (if one may, of course) meet you "out front" with a cab, or walk you to the cabstand? Nod head if so, dear.'

The second note, written in the same hand read, 'Lovely You. Had a glimpse of you one week ago, Friday last, quite late in the evening. Forgive me, but may I meet you when you have finished to-nite, please?' Both letters were simply signed 'H' and finding the author now became a major priority.

Unfortunately, it wasn't long before this promising lead petered out to nothing. Another woman who worked at the club soon came forward with a letter she had received. It was written in the same hand and in the same style and even began with the words 'Lovely You'. On her letter, however, 'H' had signed his full first name, 'Hale'. Contact was made with the American military authorities and Hale was soon traced. He was an army private now serving at a military hospital in the Midlands and had been nowhere near Southampton on the night of the murder. He was eliminated from the inquiry.

That inquiry continued but no new leads were forthcoming. The soldier seen with her in Above Bar, the one seen leaning against the Bay Tree Inn and the one seen with her in the Robert Burns were never traced. When the adjourned inquest re-opened in August a verdict of murder by person or persons unknown was returned and the cul-de-sac murder of Mary Helen Hoyles remains unsolved.

CHAPTER TEN

1945

In the early hours of 2 January Frederick Gardner was driving his taxi-cab from Bitterne towards Southampton. He had a passenger, an American naval officer, who wished to be taken to the town centre. As the cab turned into Bitterne Road, Gardner and his fare came upon a terrible sight.

A jeep lay on its side, the windscreen, steering wheel and bonnet torn off. The windscreen and bonnet had been thrown across the street and landed upon some barbed wire protecting the trading premises of Howard Brother, timber merchants. Worse still, in the road in front of the jeep lay the dead body of another American naval officer.

The police were called in and an investigation began. Photographs were taken of the scene and it became clear that the jeep had collided with a stationary lorry parked on the left-hand side of the road, facing towards the town.

The registration of the lorry was COW 583 and the police discovered that this belonged to another timber merchant but had been rented out to a firm of contractors in Netley. When they were contacted they informed the investigating officers that the driver of that lorry was Cecil Thomas George Stroud, who lived in Bitterne. When he was interviewed he explained that he had parked the lorry on some waste ground in Merry Oak Road, not far from his home, at 9.30pm the previous night. The lorry had been stolen and the first Mr Stroud knew of it was when the police knocked on his front door.

Meanwhile, the dead officer had been identified as Lieutenant Robert James Hogan who had hailed from Buffalo, New York. It was clear that whoever had stolen the lorry had subsequently abandoned it and the unfortunate lieutenant had not seen it in the darkness and run into the back of it. His watch, damaged in the impact, had stopped at 1.13, giving the exact time of the accident.

Cecil and Ronald Dear were twin brothers who had been born in Southampton just after the end of the First World War in 1918. They grew up as inseparable companions who did everything together. They went to Mount Pleasant School together, they started work together at the same establishment, Mr Ryder's office in London Road. They even had the same hobbies, both being especially interested in drawing and sketching and attended classes at the School of Art and when war broke out in 1939, they joined the RAF together. This was the first time they were separated in their lives when they were posted to different stations.

Now, in January 1945, the attachment was broken forever for their father, Ernest, had received official notice that Cecil had been killed in a flying accident. He had been shot down whilst taking part in an operation in the Middle East and afterwards sent back to England as a gunnery instructor. It was whilst on a flight there that his plane had crashed and he had lost his life. His brother Ronald remained as a radio operator, somewhere in the European theatre of war.

On 12 January, Mabel Harding of Arthur Road, Shirley, appeared before the magistrates charged with offences under the Rationing (General Provisions) Order, 1944. The story was that in July 1944, at the end of the rationing year, people were invited to change their old ration books for new ones. Mrs Harding, who was pregnant at the time, said that she had lost her old book and signed a sworn declaration to that effect after which she was issued with three emergency cards to last her for the next three weeks. She was also given a form to fill in so that she could obtain a new ration book.

Mrs Harding filled in the form and in due course, a new book was issued. However, she also produced a page torn from the old, supposedly lost book and by using that filled out a second form and received a second book. She then used one book at the original grocer and butcher she was registered with, but also registered with a new grocer and butcher so that she could use the second book. In effect, this gave her double rations until the subterfuge was discovered.

Giving evidence on her own behalf, Mrs Harding claimed that the first book had indeed been lost but that after some weeks, someone had posted it through her letter box and, as she wasn't feeling well, she was tempted to use it. The magistrates stated that this was a very serious charge and, returning a guilty verdict, fined her a total of £25 on three separate charges. She was fined £5 for failing to return a ration book to the Food Executive Officer, £10 for improperly obtaining rationed food for her household and £10 for a similar offence.

It was also in January, on the 27th, that the Auschwitz concentration and extermination camp was entered by Russian troops. Finally, the truth of the 'Final Solution' became known and horrified the civilised world.

The war against Japan was still continuing of course and on 19 February American forces invaded the island of Iwo Jima. The bloody fighting would continue until the middle of March, with a great loss of life.

The very last V2 rockets fell on Britain on 27 March. One fell in east London killing 134 people and another fell on Orpington and claimed the life of just a single person. Two days later, on the 29th, the last V1 fell on British soil when it struck Datchworth in Hertfordshire.

After securing a fourth term as US President, Roosevelt would never take office for that term because he died on 12 April and Harry S. Truman took over the office. Hitler took the death of Roosevelt as a sign that, even at this late hour, Germany would eventually triumph in the war. Eight days later, on 20 April, Hitler celebrated his 56th birthday.

On the evening of 18 April a Southampton council meeting took place to discuss the rising tide of vandalism by young hooligans within the town. Alderman Mouland, the chairman of the Works Committee, told the meeting that, on average, three or four street lamps were smashed each night. Young boys had been seen walking down the streets with catapults and airguns, which they used to smash the lamps. However, the greatest worry was that there were also adults and even servicemen in uniform doing the same sort of thing.

It was suggested that ratepayers might assist by supplying the names and addresses of those involved and teachers might give their pupils talks on how dangerous and wicked such actions were. Further, when those involved were caught and appeared in court, magistrates might impose stiffer sentences and that the names of those convicted might be published in an attempt to shame them.

It was accepted that the police were doing all they could but there simply weren't enough constables to cope with the volume of hooliganism. The suggestion was that citizen committees be set up. The matter was left unresolved, with Councillor Bascomb commenting that perhaps thinks would improve naturally once the blackout was no longer needed and the street lights could be switched on again.

April proved to be a pivotal month. On the 25th, Russian and American troops met on the banks of the River Elbe near Torgau in Germany. By the 27th, German forces in Berlin were completely encircled. The following day a disguised Benito Mussolini was captured whilst trying to escape. He and his mistress, Clara Petacci, were both shot dead and hanged upside down in Milan. On the 29th, Hitler married his mistress Eva Braun, and the following day they both committed suicide and their bodies were burned.

The war in Europe was coming to an end. On 2 May the Russians captured the Reichstag and on the same day General Helmuth Weidling, commander of the Berlin Defence Area, surrendered Berlin to General Vasily Chuikov. Two days later, German troops in the Netherlands and Denmark surrendered. However, on the 6th, German soldiers opened fire on a celebrating crowd in Amsterdam.

The final act took place on 7 May when Germany surrendered unconditionally at the Western Headquarters in Rheims. However, at 11.00pm that same day, a German U-boat torpedoed the SS *Avondale Park* off the Firth of Forth. Two people were killed in this last sinking of a British vessel during the war. The following day, 8 May, was declared to be VE Day. However, it was as late as 9 May when the only part of occupied Britain, the Channel Islands, received the surrender of German troops there.

There were, of course, many celebrations in Southampton for VE Day but perhaps one couple had an extra special reason to remember the day for Miss Brenda Lawrence of 29 Coleman Street and Chief Petty Officer William Bailey were married at St Matthew's Church. The bride was given away by her brother and her two sisters, Irene

VE Day celebrated in Southampton.

and Sylvia, acted as bridesmaids. A reception followed at which sixty people toasted the happy couple.

Meanwhile, discussions were taking place in the council chamber over the possibility of having temporary shops in the town centre. There could be no question of permanent buildings at the present time as neither labour or money was available in sufficient quantity, and if temporary ones were constructed, they would be around for some considerable time.

In June, an agreement was reached to divide conquered Germany into four areas of control. Each would be governed by the different military authorities: American, British, French and Russian. The UK began demobilisation later the same month.

Southampton was already planning for the future. In mid-June dredging operations started to provide for the extra draught of ocean-going liners. These would, in the future, cater for the holiday trade again but initially the large ships would be used to take American troops home. This would not begin, however, until the Admiralty issued an official confirmation that all German submarines had been cleared from the Atlantic.

At Alamogordo, New Mexico on 16 July the first test of an atomic weapon was conducted. Plans were already underway for a land-

Removing the town's defences – two workmen are taking up the dragon's teeth in Millbrook Road.

Welcoming home prisoners from the Japanese theatre of war.

based invasion of Japan but this successful test would give another, less bloody method, as far as the Allies were concerned, of ending the war against Japan.

Winston Churchill had proved to be a most able war leader but after so many years of conflict it appeared that the British people craved change. A general election took place on 26 July and this proved to be a landslide victory for the Labour Party. In Southampton, Mr R. Morley was the new MP with 37,556 votes, a majority of just 502 votes over his nearest rival, Alderman Lewis. The results were not actually declared until three weeks after polling in order to give time for all the forces' votes to be counted and when all the results were in the House of Commons was made up of 393 Labour MPs, 197 Conservative, 12 Liberals, 11 Liberal Nationals and 27 others. Amongst the

Mr Morley, the new MP for Southampton.

The civil defence are stood down.

new influx of MPs was a certain Harold Wilson, who was elected in Ormskirk.

There were further council discussions in July when it was reported that a suggestion had been made to scrap Southampton's trams. Though this was not, as yet, a firm plan, it was estimated that 110 extra buses would be needed to replace the trams, should the final decision be made to get rid of them.

The war finally came to a complete end in August. On the 6th, the *Enola Gay* dropped the first atomic bomb on Hiroshima. This was followed, on the 9th, by a second bomb, dropped on Nagasaki. The death toll was horrific but even after this right-wing elements of the Japanese government opposed any talk of surrender. It took an announcement by Emperor Hirohito on 15 August to say that Japan wished to end hostilities. On the same day, VJ Day was celebrated all over the world.

On 24 August, an inquest opened in Southampton to investigate a tragic story. Margaret Emma Spencer, 24, of 168 Oak Tree Road, Bitterne Park, was judged to have first murdered her child, 22-month-old Jeffrey William Spencer and then taken her own life.

The two bodies had been discovered by Margaret's father, in the kitchen of their home. Mr Spencer told the court that when he left for work on the previous Wednesday his daughter and grandson were in bed. When he returned home at 5.30pm he went to the back door, as was his custom, and it was then that he noticed a blanket had been draped over the glass panel in the door, which was locked and bolted. Using a front door key, Mr Spencer was able to gain entrance. When he did so he found that an old coat had been placed over the internal kitchen door, and sealed with tape. There was a very strong smell of gas and after forcing his way into the kitchen, Mr Spencer found the door of the gas oven was wide open. His daughter was lying on a mattress near the oven, with little Jeffrey in her arms.

Mr Spencer went on to confirm that whilst Jeffrey's father had refused to marry Margaret, he was paying money for their upkeep and he could see no reason why Margaret should have wished to kill her child and take her own life. Despite this, the jury returned a verdict of murder and suicide.

The official instrument of surrender was signed by the Japanese on 2 September onboard the deck of the USS *Missouri* in Tokyo Bay. Singapore was liberated by British and Indian troops on 5 September and on the 16th the Japanese garrison on Hong Kong surrendered.

On the morning of 14 September, Frederick Bowers, aged 60, and his wife, Louisa, 57, were both admitted to hospital suffering from gunshot wounds. The couple lived together in a small bungalow at 15a Botany Bay Road, Sholing and it was there that Louisa was shot in the right side of her head at around 8.00am. Police were called to the scene by neighbours and officers then started a search for Frederick who was found after he had run into a small copse on the opposite side of the road. As the police closed in upon Frederick another shot rang out and he was found to have shot himself in the face, fracturing his jaw. Nearby was a double-barrelled shotgun, both barrels of which had been discharged.

There had been some domestic trouble of late between Mr and Mrs Bowers, who had five grown-up children, four sons and a daughter. Only one of the children, 33-year-old Henry, lived with his parents and he made a statement to the police in which he said that he was in bed, just before 8 o'clock, when he heard his parents talking in another room. His mother came into his room, briefly, and as soon as she left, Henry heard a shot after which his mother called out his name. He went into the passageway outside his bedroom and found his mother lying on the floor, bleeding from a wound in her head. At the same time, he saw his father leaving the bungalow by the back door carrying a shotgun.

Henry helped his mother to her feet and took her out to the front gate where he shouted for the neighbours to come to his aid. It was one of them, the licensee of the Botany Bay public house, who rang for the police.

One of the first officers on the scene was Sergeant Norman who administered first aid to Louisa before she was taken to the hospital. After Frederick Bowers shot himself, he too was given first aid at the scene before being taken to the same hospital. A search of the house afterwards revealed a note, written by Frederick, which explained why he had shot his wife. Eventually, Louisa made a full recovery and Frederick was admitted to a mental institution where he began to receive treatment.

On 4 October, the final decision was made over the future of Southampton's trams. They would indeed be scrapped and replaced by a new fleet of buses. In the same month, there were joyous scenes amongst the massive crowds at the docks as hundreds of prisoners from the Japanese theatre of war arrived home.

There was some very sad news for the people of Southampton on 9 November for that was the day that the very popular Mayor, Councillor Job Charles Dyas, finally lost his battle with illness. His term of office ended at noon and at about that time Mr Dyas was attempting to write a speech of thanks to the people of the town for their support through his term in 1945. His condition grew steadily worse and at 3.00pm he was given Holy Communion by his chaplain, the Revd W. Barnes. Family and friends surrounded the bedside as the sacrament was given and just 90 minutes later, at 4.30pm, Mr Dyas breathed his last. It fell to the new Mayor, Alderman Vincent, to break the sad news to the council and, as a mark of respect, there was no further business that day.

Southampton was a town that had suffered much during the war against Germany and her allies. Many local citizens had perished both at home, during the blitz and whilst serving abroad. There was much rebuilding to do and it was clear that the post-war town would be very different to the one that heard the declaration of war in 1939.

On 31 December 1945, the Home Guard was disbanded. On the same day, the first shipment of bananas since 1939 were landed in Britain. At last it was time to look to the future.

Index